WITHDRAWN

1

THE SPIRIT OF CHINESE PHILANTHROPY

STUDIES IN HISTORY, ECONOMICS AND PUBLIC LAW

EDITED BY THE FACULTY OF POLITICAL SCIENCE
OF COLUMBIA UNIVERSITY

Volume L]   [Number 1

Whole Number 125

THE SPIRIT OF CHINESE PHILANTHROPY

A Study in Mutual Aid

BY

YU-YUE TSU, Ph.D.

New York
COLUMBIA UNIVERSITY
LONGMANS, GREEN & CO., AGENTS
LONDON: P. S. KING & SON
1912

THIS VOLUME

IS DEDICATED TO

DR. F. L. HAWKS POTT

PRESIDENT OF ST. JOHN'S UNIVERSITY
SHANGHAI, CHINA

sater

PREFACE

In this monograph the writer has endeavored to describe Chinese Philanthropy and to interpret its characteristics and ideals as he understands them. The subject is greater than can be adequately treated in a work of the present scope, but it is hoped that no injustice has been done to the subject and that further study of it may be stimulated by this presentation.

The writing was begun before the change of government in China took place. Some parts of the monograph, touching the political organization of the country may not therefore exactly fit the new conditions, but as they are true representations of conditions that obtained in the immediate past and went far into a remote past, we have allowed them to stand, as first written.

The problem of population in China in its intimate relation to social wellbeing and progress is of vital interest not only to China but also to the world. The writer's interest in it was first aroused by Professor A. A. Tenney's lectures at Columbia University. Professor E. A. Ross' book, *The Changing Chinese*, contains an illuminating study of it, perhaps the most thorough one that bears upon present conditions in China. The problem will repay further study.

The writer wishes to record his indebtedness to Professor F. H. Giddings, Professor Friedrich Hirth, Dr.

R. M. Binder and Mr. Parker Vanamee, for valuable
suggestions in the preparation of the monograph, and
to Professor E. R. A. Seligman, for assistance in put-
ting it through the press.

Y. Y. T.

CHELSEA SQUARE, NEW YORK CITY. *April, 1912.*

CONTENTS

CHAPTER III
CHARITY

I. *Care of Aged Men*

II. *Care of Aged Women and Widows*

III. *Care of Dependent Children*

IV. *Care of the Destitute Sick*

INTRODUCTION

In his great standard work *The Middle Kingdom* (Rev. Ed., 1904, vol. ii, p. 265) the late Professor S. W. Williams says with regard to the benevolent institutions of the Chinese: " In large towns voluntary societies are found, having for their object the relief of suffering, which ought to be mentioned, as the *Chinese have not been fairly credited with what they do in this line.*"

It has also been maintained in the early days of our relations with China that the native efforts in the matter of public charity are not worth much and that the spirit of benevolence was not an originally Chinese virtue. There may not be many who hold such views nowadays, but it appears that, to convince skeptical critics, the truth has to be traced back to the most ancient literature to show how, far from being introduced and fostered by western missionaries, as some feel inclined to assume, the spirit of charity to one's neighbor has originated and developed on Chinese soil itself. To prove this, it seems, there was nobody better qualified than a patriotic Chinese whose education might be expected to do justice to every side of the question. Such is Mr. Andrew Yu-Yue Tsu, the author of this essay, who combined researches in Chinese literature, carried on in seminar work under the Department of Chinese with western methods studied in the Departments of Sociology and Social Economy.

FRIEDRICH HIRTH,
Professor of Chinese.

DEPARTMENT OF CHINESE,
  COLUMBIA UNIVERSITY,
    NEW YORK, *May 10, 1912.*

CHAPTER I

CHINESE PHILANTHROPY IN THOUGHT AND PRACTICE

The Study of Philanthropy.—Philanthropy has been defined as "universal good-will," or "spirit of active good-will towards one's fellow-men, especially as shown in efforts to promote their welfare."[1] As a social phenomenon, philanthropy had originated in sub-human gregariousness and mutual aid, but its wonderful development has been achieved in human society through human consciousness. The process whereby philanthropy has reached its present status may be traced by pointing out its several stages. As an ideal, philanthropy was first regarded as a personal virtue, a quality of the pious soul, and as such received tremendous encouragement and development by a close alliance with religion. But at present, philanthropy shows a tendency to dissociate itself from religion and to occupy an independent position. The conception of it as a personal virtue is being merged into the larger conception of it as a social virtue. As a social virtue, philanthropy seems coextensive with consciousness of kind. From a narrow ideal, coinciding with family, clannish, tribal and national limitations of sympathy, philanthropy is tending toward universalism *pari passu* with the growth of sympathy. In practice, philanthropy began as a palliative for distress, as alms-

---

[1] *Webster's New International Dictionary*.. Reference History edition, 1911.

giving, grew into institutional charity, and finally became a science, variously known as scientific philanthropy or social economy. It began with emphasis upon the individual; it now seems to be laying more and more emphasis upon the social environment. Instead of aiming to improve the condition of the poor and destitute directly, it aims to do so indirectly by the improvement of such social conditions as cause poverty and destitution. It has adopted as its goal the total elimination of the causes of poverty and misery in society.[1] In adopting such a goal, and working toward its realization, the philanthropist joins hands with the sociologist, the economist, the ethicist, the statesman and other workers in other fields of human effort for progress toward a perfect society.[2]

I. PHILANTHROPY IN CHINESE THOUGHT

Philanthropy as a virtue: As a virtue philanthropy has been highly exalted by the Chinese moralists of all ages. Both Confucius and Mencius regarded it as the distinguishing characteristic of man,[3] as one of the fundamental constituents of nobleness and superiority of character.[4] Asked by one of his disciples about philanthropy, Confucius replied. 'It is to love all men.'[5]

Philanthropy natural to man: High and noble as the virtue of philanthropy is, it is nevertheless conceived of

---

[1] Devine, *Principles of Relief*, p. 181.

[2] Spencer, *Principles of Ethics,* vol. ii, pp. 432-3 Giddings, *Principles of Sociology,* pp. 420-2.

[3] *Analects of Confucius*, tr. Legge, '*Chinese Classics*', vol. i, p. 405; *Mencius*, tr. Legge, '*Chinese Classics*', vol. ii, p. 485.

[4] *Analects*, p. 320.

[5] *Ibid.*, p. 260.

as lying naturally within the capacity of every person.
Thus it is written in the *Classics:*

The feeling of commiseration belongs to all men ; so does
that of shame and dislike ; and that of reverence and respect ;
and that of approving and disapproving.   The feeling of commiseration implies the principle of benevolence ; that of shame
and dislike, the principle of righteousness ; that of reverence
and respect, the principle of propriety ; and that of approving
and disapproving, the principle of knowledge.   Benevolence,
righteousness, propriety, and knowledge, are not infused into
us from without.   We are certainly furnished with them. . . .
Hence it is said " Seek and you will find them.   Neglect and
you will lose them."   Men differ from one another in regard
to them ;—some as much again as others, some five times as
much, and some to an incalculable amount :—it is because
they cannot carry out fully their natural powers.[1]

   The spontaneity of sympathy in man is set forth in the
following lines :

All men have a mind which cannot bear to see the sufferings
of others. . . . My meaning may be illustrated thus ; If men
suddenly see a child about to fall into a well, they will without exception experience a feeling of alarm and distress.
They will feel so not as a ground on which they may gain the
favor of the child's parents, nor as a ground on which they
may seek the praise of their neighbors and friends, nor from
a dislike to the reputation of having been unmoved by such a
thing.   From this case, we may perceive that the feeling of
compassion is essential to man.[2]

   Acquirement and development of philanthropy: Apparently opposed to this view of human nature, yet not

---

[1] *Mencius*, tr. Legge, *op. cit.*, pp. 402-403.
[2] *Ibid.*, pp. 201-2.

really so, is the view of another school of ethicists, whose chief representative is Hsin-tse.   His contention is that all social qualities and sentiments, which we attribute to human nature, are not original but acquired ones.   Thus he says :

Man's nature is radically evil or egotistic ; when it is good or altruistic, it is the product of art. . . . By nature a man when hungry desires to eat, when cold, to clothe himself, when tired, to rest.   Yet to-day, a man seeing his father or brother in the same condition will desist from self-gratification in deference to his father or brother.   Such action or rather inhibition from action is against his nature, but it is in accordance with the principles of a dutiful son or of an affectionate brother and with the established morals and rights. Following nature there will be no self-restraint or deference to others.[1]

Like the other powers, the power of philanthropy is capable of development through exercise.   Thus after saying that the four principles of benevolence, righteousness, property and knowledge are natural and essential to man, Mencius continues :

Men have these four principles just as they have their four limbs.   When men, having these four principles, yet say of themselves that they cannot develop them, they play the thief with themselves, and he who says of his prince that he cannot develop them, plays the thief with his prince.   Since all men have these four principles in themselves, let them know to give them all their development and completion, and the issue will be like that of fire which has begun to burn, or that of a spring which has begun to find vent.   Let them have their complete development, and they will suffice to love and protect all within the four seas.   Let them be denied that devel-

---

[1] Hsin Tzŭ, *Essay on Human Nature.*

opment, and they will not suffice for a man to serve his parents with.[1]

State and philanthropy: Ancient ethico-political thinkers have always thought of ethics and politics as closely allied. The state is regarded as existing for the promotion of human happiness; the best government is one which is truly benevolent in its solicitude for the welfare of the people. Hence the term 'benevolent government' occurs frequently in the Chinese Classics.

Once Mencius was consulted by King Hwuy of Leang regarding Government. The king complained that inspite of his efforts for the good of his people, he failed to attract them to himself, and he wanted to know the reason for it. Mencius, knowing that the cause of the failure was the luxury of the court and its indifference to the real needs of the people gave the following pointed reply :

Your dogs and swine eat the food of men, and you do not know to make any restrictive arrangements. There are people dying from famine on the roads, and you do not know to issue the stores of your granaries, for them. When people die, you say, "It is not owing to me ; it is owing to the year." In what does this differ from stabbing a man and killing him, and then saying ; "It was not I ; it was the weapon"? Let your Majesty cease to blame on the year, and instantly from all the empire the people will come to you.[2]

Goal of state philanthropy: The benevolent office of the state must be for the elimination of material destitution among the people, and the realization of economic sufficiency, as its first duty, for without economic suf-

[1] *Mencius,* tr. Legge, *op. cit.,* p. 203.
[2] *Ibid.,* p. 132.

ficiency, there would be no possibility of spiritual progress. The picture of economic sufficiency among the
people is thus depicted :

Around the homestead with its five mow, the space beneath
the walls was planted with mulberry trees, with which the
women nourish silk-worms, and thus the old were able to
have silk to wear. Each family had five brood hens and two
brood sows, which were kept in their breeding seasons, and
thus the old were able to have flesh to eat. The husbandmen
cultivated their farms of hundred mow, and thus their families
of eight mouths were secured against want.[1]

Opposition to philanthropy: Just as philanthropy is
exalted by Confucius and Mencius as the distinguishing characteristic of humanity and as a virtue to be
cherished by all, so it is denounced by Chuang-Tzŭ, the
Taoist, as a false outgrowth of human nature and as a
disturbing factor in human wellbeing. In his writings,
there is an account of an imaginery interview between
Confucius and Lao Tzŭ, the founder of Taoism, in which
the principle of philanthropy is made to appear in the
light above described:[2]

When Confucius was going west to place his works in the
Imperial library of the House of Chow, Tzŭ Lu counselled
him, saying, "I have heard that a certain librarian of the
Cheng department, by name Lao Tan, has resigned and retired into private life. Now as you, Sir, wish to deposit your
works, it would be advisable to go and interview him."

"Certainly," said Confucius ; and he thereupon went to see
Lao Tzŭ. The latter would not hear of the proposal ; so
Confucius began to expound the doctrines of his twelve
canons, in order to convince Lao Tzŭ.

[1] *Mencius,* tr. Legge, *op. cit.,* p. 461.

[2] *Chuang Tzŭ, Mystic, Moralist, Social Reformer,* tr. H. A. Giles,
pp. 165-167.

"This is nonsense," cried Lao Tzǔ, interrupting him. "Tell me what are your criteria."

"Charity," replied Confucius, "and duty towards one's neighbor."

"Tell me, please," asked Lao Tzǔ, "are these part of man's original nature?"

"They are," answered Confucius. "Without charity, the superior man could not become what he is. Without duty to one's neighbor, he would be of no effect, These two belong to the original nature of a pure man. What further would you have"?

"Tell me," said Lao Tzǔ, "in what consist charity and duty to one's neighbor?"

"They consist," answered Confucius, "in a capacity for rejoicing in all things; in universal love, without the element of self. These are the characteristics of charity and duty to one's neighbor."

"What stuff!" cried Lao Tzǔ. "Does not universal love contradict itself? Is not your elimination of self a positive manifestation of self? Sir, if you would cause the empire not to lose its source of nourishment, there is the universe, its regularity is unceasing; there are the sun and moon, their brightness is unceasing; there are the stars, their groupings never change; there are birds and beasts, they flock without varying: there are trees and shrubs, they grow upwards without exception. Be like these; follow Tao; and you will be perfect. Why then these vain struggles after charity and duty to one's neighbor, as though beating a drum in search of a fugitive. Alas! Sir, you have brought much confusion into the mind of man."

Philanthropy unnatural to man.—Chuang Tzǔ's view of human nature is therefore diametrically opposed to Confucius and Mencius. To try to make men charitable is as much destruction of his nature and so injurious as it is to try to lengthen the legs of a duck or to shorten those of a crane. In either case, there is an attempt to

go against what has been foreordained by natural provi-
dence, and the result is suffering, physical for the one and
moral for the other.   All is well with nature, Chuang
Tzŭ would say; nature is self-sufficient, let it evolve itself
undisturbed by human artifice; this is the royal road to
complete contentment and happiness of life.   Thus he
says :

Intentional charity and intentional duty to one's neighbor are
surely not included in our moral nature.   Yet what sorrow
these have involved. . . . And the charitable of the age go
about sorrowing over the ills of the age, while the non-charit-
able cut through the natural conditions of things in their
greed after place and wealth.   Surely then intentional charity
and duty to one's neighbor are not included in our moral
nature.   Yet from the time of the Three Dynasties downwards
what a fuss has been made about them!

Those who cannot make perfect without arc, line, com-
passes and square, injure the natural constitution of things.
Those who require cords to bind and glue to stick, interfere
with the natural functions of things.   And those who seek to
satisfy the mind of man by hampering with ceremonies and
music and preaching charity and duty to one's neighbor,
thereby destroy the intrinsicality of things.

. . . And just as all things are produced, and none can tell
how they are produced, so do all things possess their own
intrinsic qualities and non can tell how they possess them.
From time immemorial this has always been so, without varia-
tion.   Why then should charity and duty to one's neighbor
be as it were glued or corded on, and introduced into the
domain of Tao, to give rise to doubt among mankind ? [1]

Destruction of the natural integrity of things, an order to
produce articles of various kinds—this is the fault of the artisan.
Annihilation of Tao in order to practice charity and duty to
one's neighbor—this is the error of the Sage.[2]

[1] *Chuang Tzŭ*, tr. Giles, pp. 101-102.   [2] *Ibid.*, p. 108.

In concluding this discussion of philanthropy in Chinese thought, we may say that the Chinese nation has always considered Confucianism orthodox and Taoism heretical.   In spite of the beauty and vigor of his philosophy and his language, Chuang Tzŭ has not succeeded in breaking the influence of the teachings of Confucianism upon the nation and its civilization.

II. CHINESE PHILANTHROPY IN PRACTICE

Historical Notices.—Chinese history has been written not as a history of a people, but as a chronicle of kings and emperors.   Hence while giving detailed accounts of royal lives, deeds and reigns, it gives meagre notices of the lives and activities and conditions of the people, and the latter, in fact, only where illumined by contact with royalty.   This being so, we find that the practice of philanthropy, so far as recorded, has been contemplated as originating with the rulers, as a function of the state, as imperial paternalism flowing downwards to benefit the people, while practically nothing is said of initiative and practice in philanthropy on the part of the people themselves.   Such a representation becomes the historians of the court, whose function is the preparation of the historical archives of the reigns and dynasties for the glorification of dead kings and emperors.   We are not therefore to infer from historical notices that the people have been nothing else than receivers of Imperial charity.   As we shall see in the following chapters, popular initiative and participation in philanthropy seem to be so prevalent in reality as to overshadow whatever Imperial initiative and participation there is in the same.

Ancient Old-Age Pensions: The earliest rulers, known as the Five Rulers (2255–2205 B. C.), were described as setting the example of nourishing the aged of the nation for later rulers:

The lord of Yü, nourished the aged (who had retired from the service) of the state in (the school called) the higher hsiang, and the aged of the common people (and officers who had not obtained rank) in (the school called) the lower hsiang. The sovereigns of Hsia nourished the former in (the school called) the hsü on the east, and the latter in (that called) the hsü on the west. The men of Yin nourished the former in the school of the right, and the latter in that of the left. . . .[1]

We may regard this as the earliest instance of Old Age Pension System sanctioned by the state.

Poor Relief : The poor are described as of four classes :

One who while quite young, lost his father was called an orphan ; an old man who had lost his sons was called a solitary. An old man who had lost his wife was called a pitiable widower ; an old woman who had lost her husband was called a poor widow. These four classes were the most forlorn of Heaven's people, and had none to whom to tell their wants ; they all received regular allowances.

The dumb, the deaf, the lame, such as have lost a member, pigmies and mechanics, were all fed according to what work they were able to do.[2]

They received the emperor's bounties, as he ordered his officers periodically to open his granaries and vaults and distribute their contents to the poor and friendless and the needy.[3]

Beginnings of Institutional Charity and Social Legislation: During the Chow dynasty (1122–255 B. C.), the state periodically gave relief to orphans in spring and summer, and during the Han dynasty (206 B. C.–25

[1] *Lî Kî*, tr. J. Legge, in *Sacred Books of the East*, ed. F. Max Müller, vol. xxvii, pp. 242, 466.

[2] *Ibid.*, pp. 243-244.

[3] *Ibid.*, p. 264.

A. D.), an emperor ordered state support of neglected children and children of poor families with supply from the public granaries. During the Sung dynasty (960–1260 A. D.) public lands were devoted to the cultivation of grains, which went to fill public granaries established in all districts; buildings were erected for the reception and care of cast-away children.[1] An emperor of the Yuan dynasty (1260–1368 A. D.) in 1271 ordered almhouses to be built for the shelter of the poor.[2] In 1659, Emperor Sun-chi issued an edict in which desertion or destruction of infants was severely condemned. He observed therein that it seemed strange to him that while the beasts of the field and the fowls of the air cherished their young, rational beings should want to destory their daughters; that the destruction of infant life was a blacker crime than robbery, for all creatures were ordained of Heaven to live.[3] In 1711, Emperor Kang Hsi ordered the establishment of foundling hospitals throughout the empire. A private hospital that was established two years after this date at Shanghai survives to this day.[4] In 1724, a government almshouse was opened at Canton; and in 1739, Emperor Kien Lung ordered it to feed 4,676 destitute persons.[5] In 1783, the same Emperor reprinted the edict of 1659, condemning persons committing infanticide to be punished with 100 blows and exile for a year and half.[3] In 1805, (9th year of Kia King) a private charities society, at Shanghai, the

[1] *Chinese Repository*, vol. xiv, p. 184.

[2] H. C. Chen, *Economic Principles of Confucius and His School*, vol. ii, p. 298.

[3] J. R. Grey, *Walks In The City of Canton*, p. 571.

[4] *Chinese Repository*, vol. xiv, p. 180.

[5] *China Review*, vol. ii, p. 91.

Hall of United Benevolence, was formed;[1] since then, it has had an unbroken career. In 1873, a proclamation encouraging care and preservation of infant life was issued by the provincial authorities of Hupeh.[2]

The above account of the beginnings of institutional charities and social legislation is far from being a complete statement of what took place during the years mentioned; it is intended only to serve as an indication of the development of practical philanthropy in China.

The poor law of China: The law of China recognizes the right to relief of those dependent persons, who may be classed as the 'worthy poor.' This right is contained in the following law :

All poor destitute widowers and widows, the fatherless and children, the helpless and the infirm, shall receive sufficient maintenance and protection from the magistrates of their native city or district, wherever they have neither relations nor connections upon whom they can depend for support. Any magistrate refusing such maintenance and protection, shall be punished with 60 blows.

Also when any such persons are maintained and protected by government, the superintending magistrate and his subordinates, if failing to afford them the legal allowance of food and raiment, shall be punished in proportion to the amount of the deficiency, according to the law against an embezzlement of government stores.[3]

The law not only recognizes the right to relief, but also stipulates that the relief should be sufficient, and that the negligent magistrate must be punished.

Ineffectiveness of the law: Good as the law is, there

---

[1] *Chinese Repository*, vol. xv, p. 402 *et seq.*

[2] Grey, *op. cit.*, p. 575.

[3] *Ta Tsing Leu Lee*, tr. G. T. Staunton, p. 93.

are serious defects in its administration. In the first place,
its enforcement would require poor-law administrative
machinery, but no such provision is made by the Imperial Government, and so its provisions merely impose
additional duties upon magistrates already burdened
with other functions. In the second place, supposing
poor relief were seriously contemplated by the magistrate, he is met by another difficulty: he must find his
own funds for it, from the same source that he usually gets
his official emoluments, from the land tax. Theoretically,
he is expected to find funds for all kinds of undertakings from this source, but because of his own insignificant official salary, of his need of paying the government
employees in his district as well as of furnishing fixed
revenue for the Provincial and Imperial Administrations,
practically he is unable to find much left for poor relief. In the third place, to increase taxation is out of
the question, so long as there remains Imperial sanction
that the land tax is forever fixed, and so long as the
people are without voice or vote in the government.[1]

Legal Status of Popular Philanthropic Institutions:
For these reasons, the excellent law has remained practically a dead letter on the statute-book. There are
government reliefs and charities, but their number is insignificant compared with those philanthropic institutions that have been organized by the people themselves and are controlled by them. These popular
institutions being under the law, of necessity, are nom-
inally under the supervision of the civil authorities, in
whose jurisdiction they are placed. There is some form
of legal incorporation, whose chief elements are approval
of the institutions by the civil authorities and their

---

[1] For further discussion of this point, see chap. v, *infra*.

promise to protect (and sometimes, financially to assist) them. But the real control of the institutions is not in the hands of the civil authorities, but in those of the people, and their support is derived almost entirely from voluntary sources rather than from official ones.

Relative Efficiency of State and Popular Control: The popular character and control of philanthropic institutions cannot be too strongly advocated. First, popular institutions give the people opportunity to be interested in social work ; they are incidentally educative agencies for the development of social responsibility in the minds of the people. A government institution is not as interesting to the people, for it is apparently far removed from their participation therein. Secondly, popular institutions supported by the public are more responsive to criticism, whether approving or disapproving, by the people, and so tend more to efficiency, than government institutions whose support is only indirectly and remotely derived from the people. Thirdly, the management of philanthropic institutions of the people is generally entrusted to the hands of the most public-spirited and esteemed persons of the locality, for the people like to see their interests promoted ; whereas, if philanthropic institutions were under state control they would generally be regarded as a part of mere official routine work at one extreme or as a part of a spoils system at the other extreme. For these reasons, it has been fortunate that most social and philanthropic works in China have been initiated and controlled by the people themselves. This does not suggest enmity between the people and the government, but it suggests the practical democracy of the nation.

Present organization of philanthropy in China: Every city or district or town has its own philanthropic

institutions, supported by the inhabitants and adminis-
tered by their representatives.	There is usually one in-
stitution in every place which is larger than any of the
rest, and this institution serves as a central organization
for the place, corresponding, in position, but only partly
in nature to charity organization societies in the cities
of America and Europe.	Thus, we have the Hall of
United Benevolence at Shanghai, the Practical Benevolent
Society at Ningpo, the Hall of Sustaining Love at Canton, the Hall of Benevolence at Chefoo, *et cetera*, all of
which are composite organizations with special departments or forms of activity varying from five to seventeen
in number.

Scope and Character of Chinese Philanthropy: In
illustration of the activities of central charities societies,
such as we have mentioned in the preceding paragraph,
we may cite those of the Hall of Benevolence of Chefoo : [1]
The seventeen forms of activities are (1) Non-interest
loans to the poor ; (2) Burial facilities for the poor; (3)
Waste-paper collection ; (4) Assisting ship-wrecked persons; (5) Fire protection ; (6) Aid to widows ; (7) Reception of deserted infants ; (8) Free supply of books to
the poor who are desirous of reading ; (9) Free education for poor children ; (10) Orphanage ; (11) Industrial school for poor girls ; (12) Refuge for the cure of
opium-habit ; (13) Refuge for the homeless sick ; (14)
Hospital work ; (15) Refuge for the poor in winter ;
(16) Free kitchen ; (17) Vaccination.

Chinese philanthropy may be divided into three general groups : I. Charity, in the strict sense of the word,
meaning disinterested aid to the poor ; II. Mutual Benefit,
or the method of relief and protection by reciprocal

---

[1] *Decennial Report,* 1882-1891.	*China: Imperial Maritime Customs
Report.	I. Statistical Series,* no. 6, first issue, p. 60.

efforts; III. Civic Betterment, or the promotion of public welfare through voluntary co-operation on the part
of the inhabitants. There are other activities which are
benevolent in nature, such as the humane treatment of
animals, which cannot be included in the above division.
But as far as the human content is concerned, Charity,
Mutual Benefit and Civic Betterment succinctly describe
the character and scope of Chinese Philanthropy.

CHAPTER II

Population and Social Well-being

Incipient Poverty : Poverty is known to exist exten-
sively in China. It is not obtrusive poverty, but per-
vading incipiency toward poverty, that obtains there. It
is expressed in the smallness of capital, in the easy pre-
cipitation of persons from frugality into destitution in
adverse times, in the lowness of wages, and in the scarcity
of luxury and comforts of life. The chief cause of this
incipient poverty, we agree with Professor Ross, lies in
the over-pressure of population upon means of subsistence. He says:

Most of the stock explanations of national poverty throw no
light on the condition of the Chinese. They are not impov-
erished by the niggardliness of the soil, for China is one of the
most bountiful seats occupied by man. Their state is not the
just recompense of sloth, for no people is better broken to
heavy, unremitting toil. The trouble is not lack of intelligence
in their work, for they are skilful farmers and clever in the
arts and crafts. Nor have they been dragged down into their
pit of wolfish competition by wasteful vices. . . . They are
not victims of the rapacity of their rulers, for if their government does little for them, it exacts little. In good times its
fiscal claims are far from crushing. With four times our number the national budget is a fifth of ours. The basic conditions
of prosperity—liberty of person and security of property—
are well established. . . . Nor is the lot of the masses due to
exploitation. . . . There are great stretches of fertile agricultural country where the struggle for subsistence is stern and

yet the cultivator owns his land and implements and pays tribute to no man. . . For a grinding mass poverty that cannot be matched in the Occident there remains but one general cause, namely, the *crowding of population upon the means of subsistence.*[1]

If the elimination of poverty is the fundamental problem of philanthropy, then the study of population is of paramount importance. Our conviction is that the solution of the problem lies in the healthy equilibration of population with the supply of subsistence and wealth, according to some worthy standard of living, through social regulation of population, on the one hand, and promotion of economic prosperity on the other.

The Population of China : No one knows exactly what is the population of China, although the Chinese government has from time to time made estimates, more or less accurate, from returns of taxation units and from enumeration of families. Probably the estimate of E. H. Parker (385,000,000) is the most reliable.[2] Similarly, the exact density of population is unknown, although as to the fact of denseness there seems to be no question. Smith says that for the plain of north China, the probable density for the more sparsely populated districts is 300 persons to the square mile, and for the more thickly-settled regions, from 1,000 to 1,500 persons per square mile.[3] F. H. King, formerly professor of agricultural physics in the University of Wisconsin, who went to China to study Chinese farming, writes that whereas in the United States land and population are

[1] E. A. Ross, *The Changing Chinese*, pp. 95-96.

[2] *China, Past and Present*, p. 30; see H. B. Morse, *Administration and Trade of China*, p. 203.

[3] A. H. Smith, *Village Life in China*, p. 19.

in the ratio of 20 acres to one person, in China they are
in the ratio of one acre to one person, and of that one
acre half is arid and unproductive. Of the real density
of cultivated land in China, America and Japan, the following summary is gathered from Professor King's
book:[1] Shantung Province has 1,783 people, 212 cattle
or donkeys and 399 swine, or 1,995 consumers and rough-
food transformers per square mile of farm land ; America's rural districts in 1900 had 61 persons and 30 horses
and mules for one square mile of improved farm land;
Japan in 1907 had 1,922 persons and 125 horses and
cattle per square mile; Chungming Island at the mouth
of Yangtse River, China, in 1902 had according to official
census, 270 square miles of land, with 3,700 persons per
square mile.

Causes of Density : We know but dimly the historic
process whereby China became populated and densely
populated as time went on. It is certain that the Chinese people are not indigenous inhabitants ; they came
from without the land. They were first heard of moving
from the north and west down the valley of the Hwang
Ho (Yellow River), and spreading thence to the other
parts of the country along natural water-courses.[2] From
the very first they were described as cultivators of the
soil. In their progress they both assimilated the inhabitants already there and drove many tribes into refuge
among the mountains of the northwestern part. We
may conclude that both congregation and genetic aggre-
gation[3] had operated to make China populous. The fertility of the land, combined with its accessibility, at-
tracted immigration and settlement, and the fertility

[1] F. H. King, *Farmers of Forty Centuries,* pp. 3-4.

[2] Parker. *China, Her History, Diplomacy and Commerce,* p. 5 *et seq.*

[3] Terms as defined in Giddings, *Principles of Sociology,* pp. 89, 91.

combined with the art of agriculture enabled people to obtain abundant subsistence, and was thus conducive to rapid reproduction. But whatever the historic process whereby China has become one of the most populous nations of the earth, we may mention some causes of prolific reproduction to-day.

Present Causes of Prolific Reproduction: 1. Rural Conditions: The population of China is largely rural, having agriculture as its main occupation. "By far the larger part of the most numerous people on the globe live in villages. . . . The traveler will be impressed with the inconceivably great number of Chinese altogether outside of the great centres of urban population.[1] For the farmer, the circuit of food-getting or the relation between labor and subsistence is the simplest, since he is able to feed himself and his family without recourse to third parties. We believe that this facility in food-getting tends to encourage the rearing of many children. Moreover, the unchanging and monotonous rural life, lacking the distracting influences of urban life, tends to confine the farmer's interests to his immediate family and thus to intensify his fondness for children. Finally, the desire for children is also strengthened by need for farm helpers, and by the wish to see one's land pass down to posterity without going out of the family.

2. *Ancestor worship*: Ancestor worship puts a premium on male progeny, since only male descendants are eligible for religious and sacrificial services before the *manes* of the departed. Naturally this tradition creates in the parents the desire to have male children, in order that their posthumous welfare may be assured. From this, perhaps, began the association of family prosperity

[1] Smith, *op. cit.*, p. 15.

with male progeny and is, perhaps, the basis of the crav-
ing for progeny, the cause for creation of large families.

3. *Early marriage*: Ancestral worship and the patriarchal family encourage early marriage. Sons live with
their parents even after coming of age; they hold no
private property until the death of the head of the family.
Marriages are arranged for by the parents, who often find
themselves under the necessity of supporting their sons'
families.   Hence, the financial check upon early marriage
among the young is absent.   Moreover, the dependence
of women upon men, the absence of self-support on the
part of women, facilitates early marriage.   Early marriage
causes rapid multiplication of population.

Effects of surplus population: The Malthusian theory
of the growth of population maintains that there is an
intimate relation between population and food-supply.
This relation may be called the equilibration between
population and food-supply.   In order to present clearly
the process as it seems to be in operation to-day in
China, its effects will be considered under four aspects.
Those extraordinary ways whereby population is usually
relieved of its surplus, such as famines, pestilence, wars,
and so forth, which Malthus emphasized, will be ignored
and more attention directed to the conditions of living,
consequent upon congestion of population.

Four Aspects of Equilibration:

1. *Population and Tillage of the Soil:* The main
source of food-supply is the soil; hence labor spent in tillage becomes the principal means of support.   The increased demand for food because of the increase of population may be met in two ways, (i) intension cultivation of
lands already under service, and (ii) extension of the area
of cultivation.   Both ways have been used in China.   It

has been observed that, whereas there are 20 acres of land for one person in America there is only one acre for one person in China, and of this one acre, half is arid and unproductive. But severe intensive cultivation has enabled one sixth of an acre of good land to support a man.[1] The continuous struggle for food has made the Chinese expert agriculturists without the aid of science.

But intensive cultivation is limited by the law of diminishing returns; it will not go beyond the point where labor fails to get its requisite compensation. New lands must therefore be sought in order to keep up with the demand for food-supply. Professor Ross witnesses that land is utilized in China as perhaps it has never been elsewhere. All available productive land is under cultivation, and there is little waste land or pasturage. He draws a vivid picture, as follows:

To win new plots for tillage, human sweat has been poured out like water. Clear up to the top the foothills have been carved into terraced fields. On a single slope I counted forty-seven such fields running up like the steps of a Brobdingnagian staircase. And the river bed, five hundred feet below, between the thin streams that wander over it until the autumn rains cover it with a turbid flood, has been smoothed and diked into hundreds of gem-like paddy fields green with the young rice. In the mountains, where the mantle of brown soil covering the rocks is too thin to be sculptured into level fields, the patches of wheat and corn follow the natural slope and the hoe must be used instead of the plough. Two such plots have I seen at a measured angle of forty-five degrees, and any number tilted at least forty degrees from the horizontal. From their huts near the wooded top of the range half a mile above you, men clamber down and cultivate Lilliputian

[1] F. H. King, *Farmers of Forty Centuries*, p. 194.

patches of earth lodged in pockets among the black, naked rocks. . . . . . .

Nowhere can the watcher of man's struggle with his environment find a more wonderful spectacle than meets the eye from a certain seven-thousand-foot pass amid the great tangle of mountains in West China that gives birth to the Han, the Wei and the rivers that make famed Szechuan the "Four-river Province." Save where steepness or rock-outcropping forbids, the slopes are cultivated from the floor of the Tung Ho valley right up to the summits five thousand feet above. In this vertical mile there are different crops for different altitudes—vegetables below, then corn, lastly wheat. Sometimes the very apex of the mountain wears a green peaked cap of rye. The aerial farms are crumpled into the great folds of the mountains and their borders follow with a poetic grace the outthrust or incurve of the slopes. . . . .

The heart-breaking labor of redeeming and tilling these upper slopes that require a climb of some thousands of feet from one's cave home is a sure sign of population pressure. It calls up the picture of a swelling human lake, somehow without egress from the valley, rising and rising until it fairly lifts cultivation over the summits of the mountains. In June these circling tiers of verdant undulating sky-farms are an impressive, even a beautiful sight; yet one cannot help thinking of the grim, ever-present menace of hunger which alone could have fostered people to such prodigies of toil.[1]

Incidentally, deforestation must result from extension of cultivation, and because of lack of knowledge of the physiographic consequences of deforestation, there has been little attempt at reforestation. To the deforestation of hillsides is due the innumerable floods of the rivers, which have caused untold suffering among the people of China.

II. *Population and Migrations:* That migrations of

[1] *The Changing Chinese*, pp. 72-74.

peoples have been caused almost entirely by physical conditions affecting food supply seems to be a well-recognized etiological fact.[1]   From very ancient times, there have been recorded movements of population in China from one part to another to relieve congestion.[2]   There must be considerable movements of population within the Chinese empire following the destructions of population in certain parts during rebellions, famines and floods, but of such intra-migrations we have no statistical knowledge.

Emigration from China to other countries has been a more conspicuous phenomenon.   Probably ten millions[3] of Chinese are now residing in foreign lands, mostly in the islands of the East Indies and in America.   This number, large as it is, is insignificant compared with the 400,000,-000 in China, but is most significant of the intense struggle for food, when taken along with the fact that the Chinese people are not strong in migratory instincts, but deeply attached to their homeland.

III. *Population and Plane of Living.:* Where the command over means of subsistence remains practically the same, a surplus of population results in general impoverishment.   Each inhabitant must work harder for his living and receive less compensation for his labor; and the final result is the reduction of comforts of life, and the lowering of the plane of living.   The real cost of an intense struggle for life does not end here, but in the deprivation of leisure time and surplus energy, which are all-essential for material and spiritual progress.   May it not be that the arrest of civilization in China, of cultural, artistic, philosophical and scientific development, in which

[1] E. Huntington, *Pulse of Asia.*

[2] H. C. Chen, *Economic Principles of Confucius*, vol. ii, p. 301.

[3] Ross, *op. cit.*, p. 106.

ancient China was so renowned, has been largely due to this deprivation of leisure time and depletion of surplus energy, because both have been absorbed in the struggle for life?

IV. *Population and Physical Energies :* A further result of the intense struggle for life is the impoverishment of vital energies, due to a combination of conditions, such as the heaviness of labor, low plane of living, insufficiency of nourishment, child-labor, unsanitary conditions, *et cetera.* An indirect witness of this impoverishment of vital energies is the habit of opium-smoking, which but yesterday claimed 25,000,000[1] as its slaves in China. Following an investigation, Mr. S. Merwin wrote:

While passing through an iron-smelting village, I noticed that the black-smiths who beat up the pig iron were regular living skeletons. They work from about five in the morning until about five in the evening, stopping twice during that time for meals. When they leave off in the evening after a hasty meal, they start with their pipes and go on until they are asleep. I do not know how these men can work. I presume that it was the hard work that made them take to opium smoking.[2]

A similar picture is given in the Philippine Opium Commission report, quoted by Professor Ross:

Absolute dullness and dreariness seem to prevail everywhere. As these two demons drive the Caucasians to drink so they drive the Chinese to opium. . . And the poor who have no leisure ? They often have no food, or so little that any drug which removes first the pangs of hunger, and later the healthy cravings of appetite, seems a boon to them. . . . The life of the indigent Chinese coolie is pain caused by privation.[3]

[1] Ross, *op. cit.*, p. 141.
[2] *Drugging A Nation*, p. 63.
[3] *The Changing Chinese*, p. 142.

Closely following exhaustion of vital energies must be early senility and high mortality. There have been various estimates regarding the death rate of adults and infants, and the average length of life in China, but until reliable census statistics are obtained, the matter remains one of conjecture. There seems to be no doubt, however, that the average length of life in China is less than in the prosperous nations of the West.

Regulation of Reproduction: Having seen the results of the equilibration of population and means of subsistence, we ask: Is there not some way whereby population and means of subsistence can be equilibrated without the attending evils, above described? Our answer to this question is conscious regulation of reproduction, on the one hand, and promotion of economic prosperity of the country, on the other.

Indirect Methods: Spencer has made clear that the multiplication of a race tends to decrease as we rise in the scale of evolution,[1] that is, in inverse ratio to the ascending individuation of its members. Applying this law of multiplication, we may reasonably expect that with the advance of civilization in China, there will be a corresponding decrease of reproductive fertility. Translated into the life of the masses, this law operates through popular education. Education increases their intelligence, which in turn multiplies their interests and wants, and so raises their standard of living. Between an over-numerous family and a high standard of living, intelligence has always decided for the latter. The maintenance of a high standard of living and of cultural achievements tends to delay the age of marriage, since the preparation of life would become more laborious and

[1] H. Spencer, *Principles of Biology.*

energy-absorbing. Especially effective in controlling reproduction and in delaying the age of marriage would be the education of girls. Education would fire them with ambitions they have never felt before, would increase their interests in the multiform activities of life, would individualize them, and would create in them the consciousness that they are more than mere sex creatures. They would not be hopelessly dependent upon men for their livelihood, and so would enter marriage as a free partner of life's sacred compact rather than be driven into it by necessity. When they have a home, they will make it not a mere feeding and breeding place, but a place for comfort, happiness and refinement.

Direct Methods : With this indirect method, there should be direct and explicit education of the people on matters pertaining to population, reproduction and social well-being. Much can be done toward the formation of sound social standards and judgments with regard to these matters through publicity agencies, such as the newspaper, public lectures, and societies. The people have not realized the importance of the problem of posterity and the heritage that is in their power to give. The motto should be implanted in the mind of every adult and parent, that quality is before quantity.

Complementary to this regulation of population is the promotion of economic prosperity, the introduction of new industries, the development of scientific agriculture and of natural mineral resources, the building of railways, the extension of commerce, the increase of industrial and political efficiency, and so forth, all of which are having splendid beginnings, so that there will be created a greater supply of economic goods at the command of the people, a greater reserve of surplus energy, and leisure time for advancement of civilization and individuation.

CHAPTER III

CHARITY

Causes of Dependence: Dependence and destitution are due to causes for which a person may be responsible or not. A person suffering from the consequences of accidents of birth, such as parental desertion, congenital deformity, mental degeneration, is not responsible for his misfortune because the causes are entirely beyond his control. In the same way, perhaps in less degree, a person is not responsible for the results of natural, accidental and social causes of dependence, such as old age, sickness, incapacity by accidents, unemployment and social prejudices. By social prejudices we mean for example such conventional habits of thought as that which prevents a woman from seeking to support herself in the economic world. Some causes of destitution, which may be distinguished from the above-mentioned by being designated personal and immoral, such as laziness, evil habits, inebriety, *etc.*, are causes for which a person is responsible. And yet, enlightened thought is coming more and more to regard even these so-called personal causes as dependent upon impersonal factors and conditions.

The Care of the Poor: It is the expression of the sense of social solidarity, whether conscious or unconscious, which urges the bearing of the burden of poverty of the few members by the community as a whole. Traditionally, there are four dependent classes in China, who are

42

[42

recognized as the worthy poor, and for whose benefit charity is largely instituted. They are the aged, the orphans, the widows, and the sick. It seems that the preference of these four classes of dependence to others as objects of public charity and care is based upon definite social judgments. The care of the aged is motivated not only by humanitarian ideas, but also by the customary regard for age which is strong in the patriarchal society of China. The care of the orphans is motivated not only by the recognition of their helplessness, but also by the value of children, engendered by ancestral worship. The care of widows is motivated not only by purely chivalrous ideas but also by the social ethic which demands that widows should neither be remarried nor earn their living independently.

Present Stage of Charity in China ; In regard to relief of the dependent classes, Chinese philanthropy has reached the stage of systematization and institutionality, of adequate relief, but not of scientific prevention of destitution. For instance, charity is ever ready to take in its care deserted infants or foundlings, and spends much energy in bringing them up; but it has not sought to correlate the social phenomenon of infant desertion with other social phenomena, such as fecundity, as cause and effect. Charity has sought to alleviate the sufferings of the sick, but has not done much for the elimination of sickness-producing conditions and causes. But the scientific stage is bound to be reached, for the principle of adequate relief must inevitably point to that goal.

I. Care of Aged Men

Attitude Toward the Aged : The attitude of a civilized community toward its worthy aged is one of deep respect and of readiness to assist in their need. For those who in their younger days have rendered public service to the nation or community, pensions, decorations and other honors are their reward. For the indigent aged there are almshouses, workshops, and homes, provided by state and private munificence. In these ways society shows its appreciation of services rendered by individuals, whether in the distinguished form of military and civil duties, or in the unrecorded form of daily work in honest pursuit of livelihood. Both forms of services benefit society, and entitle the individuals who grow old therein to the care of society, when that is needed for their comfort and happiness.

In China the aged have always received respect and deferential treatment, for filial piety is the central feature of ethics and religion, of the family and the state. The providing for the comfort of the aged who are unable to earn their living, and must depend upon the support of others, is a very ancient custom.[1] Occidental sojourners in China have observed that the faces of China's old men have the most beneficent, calm and benign expression, and have remarked that it is due to the absence of worry, since the care for aged parents is considered a sacred duty.[2] The extremely limited economic surplus of individuals leaves men in old age almost entirely dependent upon the support of their children, and were it not for this deep-rooted consciousness which regards nourishing the aged the sacred duty of the young, extensive suffering would have happened to most aged people.

Public Institutions : Private support is usually spontaneous and generous, but public institutions are neces-

[1] See chapter i.
[2] *Cf.* Ross, *op. cit.*, p. 64.

sary for supplementing relief in behalf of poor families.
Public aid takes the form of home aid or institutional
care, both of the governmental and of the popular kind.

Home Aid : In home aid, the Hall of United Benevolence at Shanghai is doing an extensive work. Care of
the aged is one of the five principal departments of this
institution. The aged remain at their own homes, and
receive monthly 600 coins. The method of administration of this aid is to have officers of the institution recom-
mend cases of indigency, or to stand as guarantee for
genuineness of reported cases, to have the cases carefully
investigated into, and after the genuineness of a case is
ascertained, to issue a ticket in favor of the applicant.
The beneficiary must be over 60 years of age, and en-
joys his benefit during good behavior until his death.[1]

Home for the Aged : At Canton, Kuangtung, there is
a government old men's Home, which according to its
records kept on stone-tablets and bronze bells is of early
origin, having been organized in 1724. Two bells within the precincts of the institution are dated respectively
1723 and 1724.[2]

The institution was described as being situated a short
distance from the East gate of the city, adjoining the
parade ground, built in rows, one story high, with plenty
of open air and space for moving about. There were in
1873, 310 inmates, five or six persons living in one room.
Besides the inmates, this institution supported partially
978 non-resident persons.[2]

The inmates must be above 60 years of age to be admitted. An admittance fee is charged which entitles the
applicant to the privilege of having his lodging there for

[1] *Chinese Repository*, vol. xv, pp. 406 *et seq.*
[2] *China Review*, vol. ii, pp. 88 *et seq.*

life.   Each inmate receives 30 catties (40 lbs.) of rice and 330 coins per month.   Every three years a suit of winter garments is distributed to the inmates.[1]

The fund for maintaining the institution came from the Commissioner of Land Tax of the province of Kuangtung, or Liang Tau, and the two magistrates of Canton were trustees; but the immediate management of the institution was said to have been farmed out.[1]

A Monastic House for the Aged: An interesting institution for aged men was maintained by the abbot of a monastery in Nankin in 1812 A. D., according to Chinese Records.[2]

It had a comprehensive and admirable regulation. Men were admitted above 70 years of age, provided they were without other means of support.   The capacity of the institution was for 160, and it was said to be full all the time.   An inmate must strictly observe the institutional life.   Once a month they were given a day to leave the house and visit friends outside; but their other absences could not be more than once or twice a month.

Four persons lived in one room; and they were responsible for its cleanliness.   Each person was provided with bedding and clothing, the use of which was regulated according to the seasons.   In winter months, fire for warming the feet was supplied.   The inmates rose in the morning with sunrise and retired with the nightfall. As a precaution against fire no lamps were allowed in the rooms.

The inmates had three meals a day of vegetarian diet, this being in accord with monastic life.   The meals were served in a large dining hall.   The superintendent struck

[1] *China Review*, vol. ii, pp. 88 *et seq.*
[2] *Tö-i-lu*, bk. iii, sec. v.

a wooden bell,—another sign of monastic life,—and the inmates assembled and together partook of their common meal, and when the superintendent got through with the meal the whole assembly was expected to rise and leave the room. One of the regulations of the institution was that the inmates being quite old, their food should be thoroughly cooked. On festival days extra food and gifts were distributed. Besides all the necessities of life freely distributed, each inmate was given 100 coins a month as pocket money. The kitchen fire was kept aglow at all hours, so that hot tea could be had when needed.

The dead of the institution were buried in the cemetery of the monastery and their names were recorded on scrolls and remembered in religious services. For the religious worship of the inmates themselves an ancestral hall was built, where the inmates could establish their own family shrines and worship there.

It is natural to infer from the above description that the life of the inmates of the institution must have been a happy one. We could imagine of the group of buildings by the side of the monastic establishment in the midst of quiet and beautiful surroundings,—as is generally the case with locations of monasteries,—possibly nestling at the foot of some hill, surrounded by tall pines and waving bamboos, embosomed in an atmosphere undisturbed by the noise and jostle of the market-places, but filled with the notes of singing birds, with the sweet-smelling incense that waft hither from the altars of the gods in the temple, and with the distant chanting of the monks in their rounds of daily exercise; and we could imagine the benign, calm and serene faces of the white-haired men of seventy and more in their rooms, in the court-yard, in the garden, conversing, reading, dreaming, or watching the flowers, the birds, the bees, contented and friendly with all nature and all men, spending the twilight of their life in peace.

II. CARE OF AGED WOMEN AND WIDOWS

Status of Woman and Civilization : The status of woman gauges the civilization of a people. In the advanced nations of the West, man and woman have each recognized the value of the other sex. Disabilities, hitherto imposed upon women are being removed. Since the beginning of the Nineteenth Century, women have come forward abreast of men, and reclaimed one after another their rights and privileges. They have the right to education, not with the expectation better to please men, as Rousseau and the 18th Century thought, but on the ground of their own satisfaction and self-development. They have free choice of professional careers and self-support; even married women hold property in their own names. They enter into marriage out of freewill; and they have the right of initiating divorce proceedings as men do. In advanced states, political suffrage has been granted to them, and they are vigorously applying their newly gained power for social betterment. Thus, step by step, the advancement of civilization is marked by the rise of the status of woman in society.

Woman in Early Times : But we need not go far back in the past to find that women were helplessly subject to masculine rule. It was not until 1848, that the married women of New York could hold property on their own account and independently of their husbands.[1] It was in 1801, that the first divorce demanded by a woman was granted in England.[2] In primitive society, woman from

[1] E. A. Hecker, *A Short History of Women's Rights*, p. 163.
[2] *Ibid.*, p. 137.

her lack of physical strength and other disabilities of sex
was at a disadvantage in competition with man. She
required his protection, and in return she became his
slave-worker. She was a slave before the institution of
slavery, as Bebel says.[1] Physical superiority became
superiority in all respects.

Widowhood : Man, having assumed authority over
woman, has for ages been the dictator of what woman
should be. The status of widows is a pertinent illustration of man-made ethics. Legouvé says:

In the past, this title of widow represents only the abasement
of the wife, the annihilation of all personality, slavery, con-
demnation, death. In our day, widowhood is freedom and
equality with man. In ancient times, every wife saw her
destiny so closely sealed to the lot of her husband, that though
a widow she still belonged to him. The tie that death had
broken for him, seemed to be drawn closer around her, and
the shade of the dead husband hovered over and subdued the
oriental woman, to drag her to the funeral pile ; on the Jewish
woman it imposed a second husband ; the Christian woman
it condemned to seclusion ; the feudal woman it delivered up
to the guardianship of her son ; the very law which left them
life refused them all power as mothers, all independence as
women.[2]

Status of Woman in China : In China, the low status
is a survival of the past, a black spot upon its civilization which has only recently begun to be wiped away.
Not that Chinese women are naturally inferior to men,
but the imperturbable customs have deprived them
of freedom and development. Without going further
into the life of women, we will study the ideas of widowhood, current in China even to this day.

[1] *Woman, Past, Present and Future.*
[2] *Moral History of Women,* bk. iv, ch. vi.

There is a book in the Chinese language, known as the *Lives of Virtuous Women*, written by Liu Hsian. It is a compilation of biographies illustrating the feminine virtues of such noted women in history as have been traditionally esteemed. For centuries this book has been considered the best text-book for young girls and young women in their preparation for their life and position in society. The first paragraph of the book quotes Confucius as saying that a woman observes in her whole life a triple dependence: at home, dependence upon the father; in wedlock, dependence upon the husband; in widowhood, dependence upon the son, there being no time when she is free of masculine supervision. Concerning widowhood, it is said that "a man has the privilege of a second marriage, but a woman never." The book abounds in stories exalting the virtue of perpetual widowhood. Two examples are here given:

In the Kingdom of Liang there was a widow, who was beautiful and virtuous. Since the death of her husband many a noble suitor had come and sought her hand; but to them all, she turned a deaf ear. Finally the King's envoy came bearing royal wish to marry her. The widow replied, I have learned about a woman's virtue; she follows one and never changes her allegiance. If she forgets her dead and puts aside her virtue in order to seek life and happiness for herself, how could she be called faithful? Thereupon the widow took a knife and mutilated her beautiful face, saying, Thus have I punished myself; I have not followed my husband on account of the child. The King hearing of this, rewarded her with gold, and called her the Virtuous Widow.

In Wei, a Lady Wong was married to a King Yu. He died, and she fearing that she might be urged to remarry, on account of her youthful age, marred her features. In her room, there came one summer, a pair of swallows and made their nest. Later, the male bird died ; but the female bird would not leave the place, and formed the habit of perching upon the arm of Lady Wong. Lady Wong was deeply touched by the bird's loneliness, and in order to identify it, fastened a little bit of silk thread upon its leg. The next summer, the same bird came to the house, but it came alone. Thereupon, Lady Wong wrote the following : Last summer you lost your mate, this summer you come alone ; Human fidelity must not be less than this.

Such devotion and self-sacrifice is worthy of the highest praise and honor in the pages of history, such noble characters are worthy of imitation by later generations. But what more wrong use of these records can be made than as instruments to inculcate in young girls and women self-effacement and submission to men. What greater injustice is there than that of forcing upon widows the limitations of perpetual sacrifice for men, without demanding proportionate reciprocation on the part of widowers. Then, because widows must live in seclusion, it becomes necessary to provide for their maintenance. In the light of the above statement, charity to widows becomes a means whereby society cultivates those sentiments in and conditions of women, which are most advantageous to men only, and so is injustice to womanhood.

Honor for Female Virtue : But we must not think that masculine selfishness is the only motive behind charity to widows. There is honor to women in China. The innumerable records in the pages of history, describing the fidelity, the heroism, the filial piety, the nobility, and the wisdom of women, as rulers, as mothers, as wives and as daughters are conscious acknowledgments of the nation's indebtedness to its women. In the same spirit, society assiduously provides for the comfort and happiness of widows during life and erects in their honor memorial arches after death.

Public Aid: Private care of aged women, as we have seen of aged men, is spontaneous. The same filial piety which considers the care of aged fathers a sacred duty considers in a far greater degree care of mothers a sacred duty. As to the widows, their families would not willingly neglect their care, since virtuous widowhood is an honor to the families cherishing it. But public aid must supplement private care on account of the limited resourcefulness of most families, as well as of the justice of the community participating in the responsibility for maintaining its own widows.

In every community, there can be found small societies or clubs whose object is to relieve widows either of the community in general or of certain groups, such as widows of scholars, widows of the laboring men, and so forth. These organizations are usually of limited operation. Besides them, there are incorporated charitable institutions, which aid widows and aged women. Of the latter, we may mention the Widows Aid department of the Hall of United Benevolence at Shanghai. In 1843, it had eighty-seven women and widows under its care;[1] in 1908, 351 persons, and in 1909 362 persons.[2] The women are divided into four classes: I. Widows who have vowed perpetual widowhood; II. Widows who are primarily poor; III. Aged women of the city; IV. Aged women of other cities. Of Class I, we found that the average age of its 100 widows is 43 years; but this number is considerably raised by a few very elderly members. The average age at which they came under

[1] *Chinese Repository,* vol. xiv, pp. 418-420.
[2] *Annual Reports.*

institutional care was 28; but the youngest was 20 and the eldest 76. Regarding the number of years they have received aid from the institution, one member who is 84 years old, has been receiving aid continuously for 58 years, another for 51 years, another for 49 years, another for 44 years, two for 43 years. The average number of years is 11.5.

In the regulations of the Hall of United Benevolence, there is a paragraph which indicates the public honor to women, spoken of previously:

If among the women there be any example of extraordinary chastity or extreme distress attended with unusual circumstances, such as the supporting of relatives, or the supporting of orphans, thereby maintaining the family, and if there be no depreciatory accounts among the villagers and neighbors, then shall a particular statement of the case be made, in order to its being recorded, in preparation for the record of merit for the prefecture and districts where it will be preserved, to the honor of chastity and filial piety.[1]

Homes are provided for aged women and widows. For example, the Home of Aged Women at Canton was reported as housing 340 inmates in 1874, besides nonresidents numbering in all 1062 individuals under its care.[2] Of the internal regulation of resident institutions for women, that of the "House of Pure Widowhood," contained in *Tö-ı-lu*,[3] is most interesting, as it shows clearly the social customs in regard to the status and care of widows in particular and of women in general.

House of Pure Widowhood: This institution at Soochow is of the nature of a cloister. It is for young

[1] Report in *Chinese Repository*, vol. xv, p. 406.

[2] Grey, *Walks in City of Canton*, pp. 525-526; Dr. J. G. Kerr in *China Review*, vol. ii, pp. 88 *et seq.*

[3] Bk. iii, sec. ii.

widows who have taken the veil of perpetual widow-hood. It provides quiet, seclusion, and sociability for the inmates. It receives not only poor widows, but also widows from well-to-do families who prefer its quiet life to that of their own homes. Once within the walls the inmates are supposed never to leave the institution again, nor to see any man, not even near relatives.

To enter the House, a woman must be a widow for at least a hundred days. This period of time is allowed in order that the widows may complete their funeral services to their dead. The candidate must vow never to marry again or to leave the House, and never to see men, except her parents and parents-in-law at the three festival days of the year. Any violation of this vow is followed by immediate dismissal from the House.

But the financial aid which the House gives to its inmates may be extended to those non-resident widows, who desire but cannot adopt the cloistered life, either because they have their mothers-in-law at home, who in old age need their services, or for some equally weighty reason.

The House is built in two sections. The inner section is the living quarters of the inmates, separated from the outer section by a wall, with a gate guarded by two old maids. Into this inner section no outsider is allowed to go. The public does not know what is contained in the outer section for the outer section is separated from the outside world by another wall, which has a gate watched by two old men.

To permit communication between the inmates and the gate-keepers, who act as errand-runners, but at the same time to obviate direct personal meeting and to avoid the inmates being seen by outsiders, a contrivance is built in the outer wall, consisting of a wooden box, like a dumbwaiter box, which is fixed and turns upon a vertical axis, so that a message placed in it by the inmates may be received by the watchmen outside by a turn of the box. This illustrates with what care seclusion of the inmates is preserved. It reflects an ancient ceremonial law, which goes as follows :

The men should not speak of what belongs to the inside of the house, nor the women of what belongs to the outside. Except at sacrifices and funeral rites, they should not hand vessels to one another. In all other cases when they have occasion to give and receive anything, the woman should receive it in a basket. If she have no basket, they should both sit down, and the other put the thing on the ground, and she then take it up. Outside or inside, they should not go to the same well nor to the same bathing house. . . . . They should not ask or borrow anything from one another. . . Things spoken inside should not go out, words spoken outside should not come in.[1]

The house supplies all the necessaries of life, such as food, lodging, bedding, furniture, clothing, small sums of money, medical care, and so forth. All these are matters of thorough regulation. In case of death, the remains are buried in the cemetery of the House, and the name of the dead is inscribed upon a scroll in the temple of the cemetery.

The children of the inmates, if any, are taken care of by the House. Girls live with their mothers, but boys live with their tutors. Girls are married on coming of age at the expense of the House; should they remain unmarried, they are treated as regular inmates. Boys are educated in the school which is attached to the

---

[1] *Lî Kî,* tr. J. Legge, in *Sacred Books of the East,* ed. F. Max Müller, vol. xxvii, pp. 454-455.

House, and should any show aptitude for a learned profession, he is specially prepared for that profession, while the rest are sent out at 14 for apprenticeship in trades.

Concluding Remarks : Although we have no exact knowledge of the number of widowed women in China, both young and elderly, we believe that it is considerable. An interesting question to ask is whether, upon the introduction of modern civilization into China and the adoption of female education and the rise of the consciousness of social justice between the sexes, the old customs regarding widowhood in particular and the status of women in general will survive or be modified. The question seems to admit of but one answer : The status of women, including widowhood, will be changed for the better. Already the traditional restrictions upon woman's work are being cast aside, because of new fields opened and demanding women. Year by year the number of young women who step out of the family circle, hitherto the only sphere of female labor, to teach in schools, to nurse in hospitals, to serve as secretaries, to work in factories, is increasing. This social change suggests a new field wherein widows may devote their time and energy : social service. As far as we know, the Christian Church invented the utilization of widows in social service. It seems to us that it is a beneficent invention both for the widows and for society. For social service, the widows in China may be trained and developed; then, instead of wasting themselves away, behind self-imposed walls of seclusion and solitude, they may go forth into society, to turn their energies of love and sympathy upon a world that sorely needs the ministry of women.

III. CARE OF DEPENDENT CHILDREN

Desertion of Infants : There are no statistics to indicate the extent of desertion of infants in China.[1] That it does exist there, there seems to be no doubt. It seems to be a social problem more serious in some parts of the country than in other parts, in some years than in others. It has been observed that infanticide and desertion are more common in the southeastern provinces than in the others, and after years of bad crops than after years of good ones. We may say that the chief causes of infant desertion are poverty and congestion of population. An official proclamation issued by the provincial authorities of Hupeh in 1873 is an illuminating document, giving the ordinary causes of this social problem. In part, it is as follows:[2]

In ancient times, the girl Ty-ying begged His Majesty Wen to permit her to sacrifice her liberty in order that her father, who was in official disgrace might be released from bondage. In another case, the girl Mulan wished to serve as a soldier in order to take upon herself the liability of her old father to serve in the wars. These instances show with what filial instincts girls of old were imbued. At the present time, we too apprehend there is no lack of daughters equally ready to sacrifice themselves to their parents or to render the names of their family as illustrious by filial acts of devotion. Such being the case, how comes it that the female infant is looked upon as an enemy from the moment of its birth, and no sooner enters the world than it is consigned to the nearest pool of water? Certainly, there are parents, who entertain an affection for their female infants, and rear them up, but such number scarcely 20 or 30 *percentum*. The reasons are either (first) that the child is thrown away in disgust because the

[1] For discussion, see E. H. Parker, *China, Past and Present*.
[2] Grey, *Walks in City of Canton*, pp. 565-567.

parents have too many children already, or (secondly) that it is drowned from sheer chagrin at having begotten none but females, or from the apprehension that the mother will not conceive again readily enough if she has to suckle the child, or lastly, in the fear that the poverty of the family will make it difficult to devote the milk to her own child, when the mother might otherwise hire herself out as wetnurse.

Now all these are the most stupid of reasons. People seem to be ignorant of the fact that no men are born from heaven without some share of its blessings, and that hunger, cold or bodily comfort are matters of predestination; so also with sons and heirs, who are even in a greater degree dependent upon the destiny of heaven, and cannot be forcibly coaxed out of it.

All that those have to do, who are unable, through poverty, to feed their children, is to send them to the foundling hospital, where they will be reared up until they become women and wives, and where they will always be sure of enjoying a natural lifetime.

With regard to the question of money or no money in the bridal casket, means or no means of bringing up a family, why, the bare necessaries of life for such children, in the shape of the coarsest gown and head-gear do not cost much. There are cases enough of poor lads not being able to find wives all their lives long but we have yet to hear of a poor girl, who cannot find a husband, so that there is even less cause for anxiety on that score.

But there is another way of looking at it. Heaven's retribution is sure, and cases are common where repeated female births have followed those where the infants have been drowned, *i. e.*, man loves to slay what Heaven loves to beget and those perish, who set themselves against Heaven, as those die who take human life. Also they are haunted by the wraiths of the murdered children and thus not only fail to hasten the birth of a male child but run the risk of making victims of themselves by their behavior.

The real reasons why girls suffer the consequences of poverty more than boys do are, (1) girls, being forbidden by custom to be wage-earners, are a heavy liability to their families, while boys are an asset in the economic struggle; (2) girls will leave their own homes and become members of outside homes, while boys remain members of their own homes and hand down the family-heritage; (3) ancestor worship requires male officiates, and so boys only can satisfy the religious demands of filial piety. In short, girls are more negligible than boys, because their social value is less than that of boys. This is a vicious judgment, born of medieval thought, and the social ethics of to-day demands its eradication.

Public Care of Dependent Children: Public care of dependent children consists of partial aid for children in poor families, and institutional care of foundlings. The first method is always preferred, wherever possible, for it preserves the home and the natural parental and filial sentiments. The next preferred method in the case of foundlings is to provide for as much home life as possible by placing them out among different homes. This is not adoption by these homes, for the children are still in the possession and care of the institutions placing them out, and it becomes adoption only after due legal transfer of right of possession from the institutions to the homes. The last method to mention is institutional care, where a number of foundlings live together with wetnurses under one roof.

Home Aid: Partial home aid is undertaken by voluntary societies in a community. Its objects are to help poor families bear the burden of their children, and thus obviate breaking up homes, and to remove the necessity of mothers working without a sufficient period of convalescence after child-birth. The amount of aid depends upon circumstances.   Ordinarily monthly supplies of food and money are given for five months after the birth of a child.   It is argued that the first five months constitute the most trying period for poor parents to keep their infants.   By the end of the five months there will have developed the tie of affection between the parents and the infants, too strong to be easily broken.   In extraordinary cases special aid is given.   Such cases are: (1) children upon whom the continuation of the family name depends ; (2) children whose mothers die at their birth ; (3) children adopted when very young by outside families.   In such cases the aid continues for three years.   Societies for protection of infants have definite areas of operation, corresponding to those of villages or wards of towns and so forth.   In this way local spirit or neighborhood feeling is utilized.   This point is illustrated in the following statement, made by a founder of a local society:

In the 23rd year of Tau Kwang (1843), I discussed the matter with residents within a radius of ten miles, urging the formation of an infants protection society to counteract the misery of poverty.   Since the formation of the society, we have successfully prevented infant desertion within the district. Monthly aids are given in every case of need for five months. Each member of the society not only pays a membership share of 360 coins a year, but also makes the promise never to desert infants.   The society has existed for ten years and each year there were from seventy to a hundred cases taken care of.   But the moral effect of such a society is far greater than the material aids.[1]

Placing-out System : The Foundling Hospital of Shanghai[2] receives foundlings, but instead of keeping them in

[1] *Tö-i-lu*, bk. ii, sec. i, p. 13; *cf.* F. Hirth, *Ueber gemeinnützige Anstalten in China,* p. 19.

[2] Report in *Chinese Repository,* vol. xiv, pp. 177-195.

one public institution sends them out to the homes
of wetnurses for care.   At the headquarters of the
institution, foundlings are received, examined and registered.   The points specified in the registration are :
(1) name and date of birth,—this being known from
written information attached to the foundlings, which
parents are usually anxious to give ; (2) physical condition, such as conditions of health or disease, perfectness
or defects of the limbs, the senses, etc. ; (3) lines and
fashion of the finger marks, for identification ; (4) the
clothing in which the foundlings are received.   A ticket
is next made out for each foundling, and the infant is
then assigned to a wetnurse.   The placing-out system
requires vigilant inspectors of the infants placed-out
and of the wetnurses, and so the institution provides as
follows : [1]

One of them to take charge of the records and registers, the
receiving of infants, the allotment of nurses, the giving out
the children's tickets, and the receiving and dispensing of
money.   It is requisite that all these be recorded minutely
and carefully.   The other, to make investigations, daily to
give out the things which may in turn be requisite, and taking
in his hand the infants' record, to go around to the place appointed for each; first to examine the child's ticket, then to
take cognizance of the nurse's diligence or neglect, and
whether the child be fat or thin, which is upon the spot to
be entered into the record, in readiness for the First and
Fifteenth days of the month, when the directors shall examine
and verify, and dispense praise or blame.

The choice of wetnurses, which is deemed very important is thus regulated :

[1] *Op. cit.*, p. 184.

The most important thing in the nourishing of the infants is the hiring of wetnurses. . . If there be any one who wishes to take this function, either her own husband can come to the office and announce her name, or a relative or neighbor must come and be security for her. The officers of the Hall must then examine whether she really is properly qualified for the function or not, and shall then enter her name upon the record; when infants come, they are to be distributed successively to the nurses.[1]

Serious negligence on the part of nurses is treated as a criminal offence.

Adoption of Foundlings: Approximately three fifths of the foundlings live, and the rest die either when received or afterwards. Of the living, three fourths ultimately are adopted into homes, and one fourth remain under institutional care. Concerning adoption, the institution provides as follows:

In the transfer of children, it is only requisite with regard to the boys that they legitimatize into some family; beyond this there is no further need for anxiety. But as regards the girls, there is great fear of their being bought as concubines, or bought and sold again with other similar abuses.[2]

Hence adoptions must be accompanied by sufficient guarantee of good faith and done through legal form:

The tickets or documents for the adopted children shall be drawn out in duplicate. The one shall be the bond for the receiving of the child, which shall be laid by in the institution, and the other the agreement of the transfer, which shall be given to the family adopting the child. These shall be stamped with the official seal of the Sub-prefect.[3]

Concerning the disposal of those who are not adopted

[1] *Op. cit.*, p. 185.   [2] *Ibid.*, p. 187.   [3] *Ibid.*, p. 186.

by families, our information is limited to a general rule, which runs as follows:

When a child has reached the age of three years, it is then able to eat and drink, to run and walk by itself and if, as hitherto, it is unadopted by any one, the said child shall receive a ticket, and be again taken into the institution, where there shall be hired nurses to take charge thereof.[1]

Administration : From the history of the institution, it seems that the officers were originally elected by the subscribers, and approved or authorized by the civil officers. Those persons were elected, who had shown themselves most energetic promotors or were most able financially to be promoters of the interests of the institution. These were positions of trust and honor. As the business of the institution became exacting and voluminous, executive officers were selected who could give entire time to the work, while the honorary officers became the directors and examiners of the records of the institution. The directorate seems to be self-perpetuating. The honorary offices descend from father to son, and from friend to friend of one's own choice. This policy seems to have been adopted on account of its practical advantages. It insures the continuity of the institution and promotes its efficiency, since neither sons nor friends would willingly abuse the honor and trust by neglecting the responsibilties of the offices. There are recorded cases in which sons unable to receive the offices that had descended from their fathers, were relieved of their responsibilities.[2]

Finances : The efficiency of management of philanthropic institutions may be illustrated in the methods

[1] *Op. cit.*, p. 187.   [2] *Ibid.*, pp. 180-182.

used for raising money.   One of the commonest methods
is known as the benevolent ticket :

It is now decided that one benevolent ticket shall be valued
equal to 360 coins, and that these shall be collected according
to the four seasons.   One person may write several tickets, or
several individuals may join together for one ticket, or all the
members of a household, both the family and domestics, may
subscribe to a corresponding number of tickets, or may call
and invite friends and relations to join in any number of
tickets. . . . According to the seasons, the tickets shall be
taken and the money called for, the period of three years com-
pleting the term.[1]

The tickets are authorized by the civil officials, and
are of the following form :[2]

Having received the sub-prefect's order to take charge of the
Foundling Hospital, we have agreed to raise a subscription,
and now beg to request you (naming the person) dwelling at
(place of residence) for a voluntary subscription of (number
of) tickets, the aggregate amount of which will be (amount
in coins).   Year, date.

Accompanying the invitation to subscribe is an essay of
moral persuasion, of the following nature :

If, for the extension of kindness to our fellow-creatures and
to those poor and destitute who have no father and mother,
all the good and benevolent would give one coin, it would be
sufficient for the maintenance of the foundlings one day.   Let
no one consider a small good unmeritorious nor a small subscription of no avail.   Either you may induce others to subscribe by the vernal breeze from your mouth or you may your-
self nourish the blade of benevolence in the field of happiness,
or cherish the already sprouting bud.   Thus, by taking your

[1] *Op. cit.*, p. 190.   [2] *Ibid.*, p. 191.

endeavors to accomplish your object, you may immeasurably
benefit and extend the institution.[1]

The merit of the 'benevolent ticket' system is that it
puts the participation in philanthropy within the capacity
of the ordinary people, who have little surplus to spare,
while at the same time it places no limit to the gener-
osity of the more capable.   It democratizes philanthropy.
Thus, during one year, 4586 tickets were subscribed by
1272 persons, of whom the 26 largest subscribers took
half of the number of tickets, and the remaining 1246
persons the other half.[2]

State Encouragement: Realizing the value of philanthropic institutions, the Government of China is in the
habit of encouraging their efforts by public recognition
of their services and by awards.   The following is an
example:[3]

Yung-ching, 2nd year, 4th Intercalary month, 28th day.   The
following edict was issued to the Prefect and Sub-prefect officers of Shun-tien Fu:

Outside the Kwang-ning gate of the capital there has here-
tofore been the Pu-Tsai-Tang, or Hall of Universal Benevolence, where all aged, diseased and destitute persons might find
an asylum.   Those who had the control of the work, invariably
delighting in virtue, well merited commendation, and His Majesty Kang Hsi gave them an inscribed tablet in order to lead
onwards the love of virtue.   You who have the official charge
of the place, ought also constantly to give them commendation
advice in order to stimulate and excite them. . . .

And we have heard that within the Kwang-kin gate there is
a foundling hospital, where all those infants and children, who
cannot be nourished and brought up are received during a
course of ten years; it has reared and settled many.   The

---

[1] *Op. cit.*, p. 191.   [2] *Ibid.*, p. 192.   [3] *Ibid.*, p. 177.

nourishment of the young and the maintaining of orphans being an exaltation of virtue of a similar nature with the supporting of the infirm, and compassionating of the aged, and a thing which in common practice of the world is difficult, we both praising and delighting in it, have especially granted a door-tablet and also make a gift of money, in order to manifest our own inclinations and to commend and lead the way in pecuniary aid to its support by our people. . . .

Institutional Care: As an illustration of institutional care where the dependent children are housed in one place we may describe the Foundling Hospital at Canton.[1] As this is a state institution light will be thrown upon others of its kind at the same time.

The institution was described as being situated a short distance from the city of Canton, built upon somewhat elevated and rolling grounds. The buildings were one story high and arranged in rows with alleys between, opening into a central street. Each row of rooms was supervised by a woman overseer. The whole group of buildings was surrounded by a wall. At one time it was said to have employed 980 wetnurses, of whom 200 resided in the institution, and the rest were non-resident. About ten or twelve infants were received every day. To dispose of its charges, the institution would daily exhibit the children for the inspection of persons who wished to adopt them. The adoption fee would be divided among the wetnurses and the other servants of the institution. The institution derived its funds from the provincial treasury, and was under state supervision and management.

Modern Methods: In recent years modern methods have been introduced into Chinese philanthropy. Of

[1] Dr. J. G. Kerr, "Native Benevolent Institutions of Canton," in *China Review,* vol. ii, pp. 89-91.

the newer type of institutions, the Home for Orphans
at Shanghai is an example. It has been in existence
for about ten years, and has recently moved into its
new home in a suburban village. It receives boys
and girls of all ages up to 16 years, and is equipped with
farms, orchards, school-rooms, workshops and play-
grounds. It teaches the boys farming, horticulture,
fruit-raising, care of trees, carpentry, furniture-making,
printing, photography, and other manual trades, and the
girls, machine-sewing, tailoring, embroidery, laundry,
music, kindergarten work, and so forth. At the time of
its last report there were ninety-nine boys from five to
nineteen years of age, and thirty-seven girls from six to
sixteen years of age. It has an enlightened aim, to make
out of the children men and women independent and
useful in society.[1]

IV. CARE OF THE DESTITUTE SICK

Public Health : The presence of sickness in a community can generally be accounted for by the unsanitary
condition of life, overtaxation of physical energies, and
lack of proper medication, For the individual, an added
factor exists, that is, the chance of communication. For
the eradication of sickness, therefore, prevention by the
improvement of sanitation and restoration of life-energy
is more important than mere medicinal remedy ; and
social effort rather than individual effort alone is powerful enough to accomplish it. But prevention depends
upon scientific knowledge of the causal relation of sanitation and health, and of the origin, communication and
cure of diseases. The impetus behind sanitary movements and preventive measures, which obtains to-day in

[1] Report of Home for Orphans, 1910.

Occidental nations is largely based upon this scientific knowledge, and the seeming apathy toward sanitation and toward diseases in the past is largely a reflection of helpfulness on the part of society to cope with them, the lack of confidence of conquering them due to ignorance of their causation, communication and cure.

Public Responsibility : In China, social responsibility of public health is sufficiency recognized but the importance of sanitation is inadequately realized because there is lack of scientific knowledge on the matter. The consciousness of social responsibility for health is shown in the existence of public hospitals for the care of the destitute sick, the distribution of medicine to the poor, public aid in the event of deaths of the needy. To the poor and the laboring class, sickness, unless temporary, is ruinous. They lack the means to command efficient medical treatment, they lose their time and health which are their most valuable possessions. A prolonged sickness may cause unemployment or neglect of the fields and plunge them into destitution. Thus, the directors of a public dispensary at Shanghai, after speaking of the sickness-begetting conditions of the fields in which the laboring men have to work in the summer and the unhealthy conditions in which they usually live said in a report :

The well-to-do get their own doctors, but if the laboring and the poor be exposed to pernicious influences and become sick, they are unable to procure medical aid, and their diseases speedily become severe. This state of things having come to the knowledge of several benevolent individuals has excited their compassion and sympathy. . . . Now it is more meritorious and praiseworthy to attend to persons while they are alive than to afford coffins for them when they are dead. . . . [1]

[1] Report of the Public Dispensary, in *Chinese Repository*, vol. xvii, pp. 193-199.

The free Dispensary: The public dispensary is the common form of relief. It is open daily or on appointed days, throughout the year or for appointed seasons. It is supported by voluntary contributions. Those dispensaries which are open for appointed days and seasons are generally able to obtain the voluntary services of the doctors while those requiring resident doctors, have to pay for their services. A subscription appeal sent out by a Public Dispensary at Shanghai furnishes some information about its work:

We respectfully notify the subscribers (that the public dispensary is attached to the Hall of United Benevolence, that it was open for three months during the last summer, that for each appointed day, it treated more than a thousand patients, that it is entirely dependent upon voluntary subscriptions, that for the present year's work it is again appealing to the merchants and scholars who delight in the works of charity). We respectfully request the lovers of virtue and promoters of benevolence to open their purses and afford relief to the sick poor and by accumulating grains of sand we shall form a pyramid. Thus whitened bones will be clothed with flesh and the well-nigh dead restored to life, the sick will be healed and immeasurable happiness diffused abroad.[1]

Sick Asylums: There are asylums where stranger who have fallen ill are sheltered. Admittance is free, but the asylum is legally free from responsibility for the inmates whatever should happen. For this purpose, a written agreement is made by the person who sends the inmate to the asylum, as follows:

We, the undersigned, having discovered at .... of the city a stranger, who is sick and destitute, on the .... day of the month, and having ascertained him to be a native of ......,

[1] *Op. cit.,* p. 197.

aged ...., without relations in this city, and having received the permit of the magistrate, send the person to you to be cared for. We fill this blank and promise to take the person away, should he get well, so that the Asylum may not be held responsible.[1]

Isolation of the Diseased : Persons suffering from contagious diseases, so far as known, are isolated. This is the case with leprosy in the southern part of China. Lepers live in colonies by themselves.[2] But isolation is not absolute. For example, in the colony, the inmates are allowed to marry and beget children. By reproduction the colony eventually becomes a centre of population, and so an economic unit, and as such could hardly be completely isolated with the rest of the economic world. Thus it is said that the members of the colony made ropes, twine, sandals and other articles of daily use and offered them for sale in the cities, in order to make a living and feed the children. We do not know whether leprosy is an inheritable disease, but it is an obnoxious idea to think that lepers should be allowed to reproduce themselves, and thus perpetuate the colony. But the description applies to the situation forty years ago. Conditions may have changed.

Care of the Defective : As regards persons suffering congenital defects, such as the blind, the deaf, the dumb, the feeble-minded, the insane, and so forth, it seems that very little is done for them through public institutions. There are here and there institutions that receive them and give them a bare living, and there are workhouses, where they are engaged in profitable industries.[3] Ac-

[1] Record of the Asylum for Strangers, Shanghai, in *Tö-i-lu*, bk. iv, sec. vi.

[2] Grey, *Walks in the City of Canton*, pp, 688-691.

[3] *Ibid.*, p. 523.

cording to an Occidental observer, the probable reason
of inaction is that the Chinese labor under an impression
that all blind persons have either in the present, or in a
former state of existence committed sins of heinous
nature, and for which by the deprivation of sight they
are undergoing a well merited punishment.[1] Hence the
lack of sympathy for their sufferings. There is, perhaps,
some such mythological thinking in the minds of some
people when they meet a blind man deprived of his sight,
or a lame man limping with crutches, or a dumb person
manipulating his fingers, or a mental defective acting in
a silly manner, or an insane person raving as if possessed
of the devil. But we believe that there is a more fundamental reason to account for the apathy toward these
unfortunate classes, than mere superstition.

It is ignorance. It is ignorance of what to do with the
blind, the deaf, the dumb, and the insane that discourages
charitable activity on their behalf. For a normal person
in distress, there is hope and reasonable expectancy that
some day a self-respecting, independent and desirable
person will be made by environmental aid. This hope
prompts charitable activity. Abnormal persons, whether
defective in outer limbs or inner organs are thought to
be hopeless cases, and so little is done for them.

The remedy for this apparent but not real apathy toward these unfortunate classes of abnormal and defective
persons is to be sought in the introduction of scientific
knowledge concerning them, their treatment and care.
On the one hand, society needs to know that many congenital and mental defects are inheritable and constitute
real degeneration of the racial stock. The earlier they
are eliminated the better for the race; and the elimina-

---

[1] Grey, *op. cit.*, p. 523.

tion may be accomplished with kindness to the unfortunate persons, and without hurting the moral sensibility of society.   On the other hand, society needs to be informed that the care of the defectives is far from being a hopeless work.   By special methods of training and supervision they may be made to earn their own living, and so reduce the burden of care upon the community, and may be given a happier and fuller life than their handicaps would otherwise have allowed them to enjoy.

Free Burial : Closely allied with the care of the destitute sick is the free burial of the poor and the distribution of free coffins.   It is a very active form of charity. The Hall of United Benevolence in the twelve months of 1908 distributed 578 coffins for adults and 867 coffins for children, and at a branch office in the same city, 631 coffins for adults and 158 coffins for children.   In its free cemetery it buried during the same twelve months 1506 adults and 3796 children.[1]   There may be various reasons to account for this activity, such as religious awe of death, superstition concerning the repose of the spirits of the dead, and other mythological reasons, but the proximate reason is the practical necessity for the work.

Need of a National Health Campaign : A much-needed campaign in China is for sanitation and positive pursuit of health.   To show what powerful social effort is available in China, we need only cite the present crusade against opium-smoking.   Thus, Professor Ross writes,

When Pekin allowed ten years for the cleansing of the land from the opium habit, it little dreamed of the enthusiastic response its initiative would call forth or of the rising spirit of patriotism that would come to its aid.   The accomplishment of the last five years elapsed has surpassed all anticipations.

[1] Report of the Hall, 1909.

The production of opium in China has certainly been cut down sixty or seventy per cent, and the reform leaders even insist on eighty per cent. Millions of smokers are breaking off because the price of the drug has risen clear out of their reach.

A national conscience is beginning to show itself and the slave of the pipe is put to the blush. It is now worth while to make the smoker carry his purchased opium in his open hand and wear his permit on a big wooden tablet that he cannot conceal. No one has a greater horror of " losing face " than the Chinese, and there is hope that the rising generation will shrink from opium as they shrink from a cobra. [1]

The virility of the opium crusade is clearly due to publicity given to the matter, exposure of the evils, and the consequent formation of a sound constructive public opinion and aggressive policy. The agitation for sanitation and health will be equally virile, given similar conditions.

[1] Ross, *The Changing Chinese,* pp. 169, 171.

CHAPTER IV.

MUTUAL BENEFIT

Mutual Benefit and Social Consciousness : Mutual benefit is an essential factor in Chinese philanthropy. There is a readiness among the people to combine in in order better to relieve one another's burdens in distress, a tendency to co-operate in dealing with want and misfortune and other adverse conditions, which constitutes a distinct social habit. Undoubtedly the tendency to co-operate in philanthropic undertakings is re-inforced by the habits of co-operation engendered in economic activities, such as the trades guild, and by consciousness of kind developed within particular groups, such as the clan or community. Thus men of the same clan or community more readily enter into association for mutual benefit than men of different clans or communities, and in the same way, members of the same trade more readily enter into association for mutal benefit than members of different trades. In other words, mutual benefit in philanthropy is an expression of social consciousness, and the degree and extent of the former is determined by the intensity and extent of the latter. If we conceive of social consciousness within a society as unevenly distributed and concentrating around numerous points which represent the numerous interests and objects for which people associate themselves, and if we conceive of it as ever tending to spread outward from these points, through friendly social interaction and co-ordination among the different minor social groups and interests until it permeates society generally, then we can think of mutual benefit as at first limited within definite areas such as the clan, the village, the particular trade-guild, and so forth, but as finally overflowing the limitations, and spreading throughout the nation.

Value of Mutuality : The value of mutuality in philanthropy cannot be overestimated. It alone may not be a sufficient agent in the elimination of distress and want, but it is a constructive agent because it recognizes the principle of justice, and utilizes the consciousness of social solidarity. Although it is a corporate functioning, mutual benefit cannot swamp individual responsibility. Although it is a charity, it does not compromise personal dignity; and although it is giving of aid, it does not pauperize the receiver.

To study this important phase of Chinese philanthropy, we will examine its clearest expressions in the clan organization, in the village community, in the voluntary associations for mutual benefit, and in the trades and crafts guilds.

I. The Clan Organization

What it is : The clan is a consanguinity group, observing patronymic descent. The families of the clan acknowledge a common male ancestor or ancestors, whether real or adopted, and are thereby held together and known by the common family name. Genealogical records are carefully kept in order both to substantiate claims of clan privileges, and to regulate the degree of kinship.

Clans send out off-shoots in the manner of trees. The larger branches trace their origin to the trunks, and the smaller branches trace their origin to the larger branches

and only indirectly to the main trunks. But the ambition
of a clan is to trace its ancestral line as far back as possible, terminating it in some well-known personage in history, and to locate its original home, to which it may
look back with pride.

Localization : A clan tends to localize, that is, to
strike root in the ground which it occupies. The localization is initiated by acquirement of estate. Time
strengthens the bondage to the locality through burial
of the dead, presence of ancestral tombs, establishment
of ancestral halls, maintenance of ancestral worship, identification of economic interest with the locality, and the
weight of tradition.

As conditions are more favorable for these achievements in rural than in urban districts,—*e. g.*, a rural district offers greater possibility for complete identification
of economic interest with locality than an urban district,—and as the relatively unchanging conditions of a
rural district offer less disturbance to the process of
localization than the relatively changing conditions of
an urban district, we find clans better localized in the
rural than in the urban districts. Localization is conducive to complete organization, and so we find clans re-
tain their solidarity as long as they remain in rural districts, but begin to disintegrate when subjected to urban
influences. But a clan organization seldom disintegrates
completely as long as there are living members. It is
kept up by the establishment of a rural home, where the
ancestral hall is built, and clan burial ground laid out. To
this home members return for reunions, usually on special
occasions for worship of ancestors.

The Social Value of Clan Organization : Whatever
the intrinsic value of a clan organization, we find it ren-
dering distinct services for social well-being in China,
owing to the presence of peculiar political conditions.

One such service is the maintenance of law and order in the country. The political government of China hitherto has been generally weak and unaggressive in the maintenance of law and order in the land, and were it not for the completeness of the organization of the people into clans, there would have existed conditions different from those that have hitherto existed in the country. The traditional law-abiding nature of the people, despite the apparent absence of governmental machinery, is explained by clan solidarity, working itself out in a system of legal responsibility of members of a family for one another.

Another service, which the clan renders is its promotion of co-operative spirit in social life. The clan trains the members to think of personal welfare in terms of social welfare, and inculcates in them the consciousness of social responsibility. The training may be narrow, but it is thorough; and in the absence of social training through national functioning, as has been the case in China until recently, the clan mode of life has been the only sphere which offered preparation for true social life, by the formulation of social habits and ideals.

There is some disadvantage to the nation in clan organization for its tendency to produce a narrow spirit of clannishness, which may prevent the development of national consciousness, and so weaken national solidarity. But this influence is much exaggerated. In the first place, clans have never been so completely isolated as to produce excessive intolerance. Trades and industries draw men from different clans, and so tend to counteract exclusiveness, by the creation of new bonds through economic interest. Urban conditions have created common civic interests among inhabitants, without regard to clan affiliations, thus tending to neutralize clannishness. The innate business instinct of the people has caused the members of different provinces and cities to travel widely and to settle in strange provinces and cities. This extends sympathies, and wears off provincialism. The system of Imperial literary examinations which were held until recently at regular and frequent intervals, at important provincial and national centers, brought together scholars from widely separated localities, and their common profession easily facilitated intercourse and exchange of ideas, and thus helped to create nation-wide sympathies and consciousness. Further, we may say that whatever clannishness and provincialism there has been in China may be as much due to geographical isolation and absence of easy communication between different parts, and to the immediate consequence of diversification of dialects and customs, as to the clan organization itself, and perhaps more due to the former than the latter.

Clan Charities: A clan possesses an estate in common. Because the estate is common property it is inalienable. It may have been handed down from some generous ancestor, or acquired by public subscription. It consists usually of grain-producing land; the rentals and grains produced therefrom are for the support of public interests, such as the maintenance of the ancestral hall and worship. Further, the common property serves as a store of wealth which in time of bad years is distributed or loaned to families to relieve them from want, and may also be used during ordinary times to help unfortunate members, widows, and poor scholars. We have the historic record of a case of clan charities, that of the Van Clan, which dates back as far as 1064, and presumably survives to this day. Such continuity through long periods is not uncommon, as clan records are carefully kept and relationships religiously maintained. We recall the sur-

vival of the clan of Confucius to this day, without break
through 75 generations, that cover a period of 2462
years,[1] the larger part of which is still residing around
the original home; and we also recall the survival of the
clan of Mencius, originating with Mencius, in 372 B. C.

The Van Clan Estate :[2] The records show that there
was an ancestor of the Van Clan, who purchased 1000 mow
of land (about 210 acres) in order to feed his own folks.
This man's father had worked toward this end but it was
the son who realized the plan and secured state recognition for the establishment of his estate. This was in
1064. Regulations were drawn up for the administration
of the estate; but further additions and changes were
frequently made as years went by, owing to the increase
of the clan population. Thus there is on record this
statement :

According to ancient custom, distribution of rice was equal,
with extra gifts for marriages, education of children and Imperial literary examination. Later, there was reduction of
land, increase of taxation and large growth in the number of
descendants. For each individual in the beginning, there are
30 individuals now. Hence per-capita distributions have to be
reduced, and the extra gifts discontinued. Other causes for
the addition and change of regulations are the variations in
the profits from the estate, and the changes of abode of the
clan population.

The Van Clan estate consisted of farm lands, farming
implements, a granary, and some living houses. The
lands were rented to farmers, who retained a fixed per-
centage of the annual produce and returned the rest to
the estate. The farmers were given the use of the public

[1] E. H. Parker, *Studies in Chinese Religion,* p. 176.

[2] *Tö-i-lu,* bk. i, sec. i.

implements of cultivation. The produce, largely consisting of grain, was stored in the public granary. The
houses were rented to farmers at moderate rates, and in
the case of poor families, rental was free. For the repair
of these houses, whenever necessary, the families occu-
pying them were held responsible, unless they were poor.
No destruction or alienation of public property was per-
missible.

Objects : The objects of having the clan estate were to
relieve the clan-members from poverty and destitution,
to encourage the education of the young, to reward virtue, such as filial piety and virtuous widowhood, and to
maintain the solidarity of the clan, comprising both the
dead and the living.

Administration : The first administration was appointed by the founder of the estate. Whether this ab-
ministration became self-perpetuating, or whether it was
coincident with eldership in the clan or with a part of it,
so that there would be no doubt as to who should have
the control of the administration in succeding generations, we are not informed. In all probability the latter
was the actual arrangement, judging from consensus of
custom.

The officers of administration seem to have held their
offices subject to the approval of the clan. A rule of
1083 provided that they could be impeached in case of
suspected abuse of authority or dishonesty; and a rule
of 1095 provided that this impeachment should go
through legal channels, with its entire technique, such
as evidence, witnesses, *etc.* Nevertheless, while in office,
the administration exercised absolute power, with which
even the right of eldership could not interfere; and the
personal right of officers, even under impeachment, could
not be reduced in any way. These rules indicate recog-

nition of the personal immunity of officers, the unlimited
character of delegated powers, and the responsibility of
the administration to the clan.   On the other hand, if
the administration showed good management, through
the annual and semi-annual reports, the officers were
rewarded with gifts of rice.   Public business meetings
were called at the Spring and Autumnal sacrifice.

Distribution of Aid : Regular distribution according to
the earliest rules (1050) consisted of rice and cloth for
every individual in the clan.   An adult received a quart
of rice per day and a roll of cloth every year.   The head
of each family submitted a monthly estimate of its
proper share to the managers of the estate, who after
verifying it would give the desired amount.   Of the
minors, the absentees and the servants, there were special
rules.   A rule of 1050 stated that a child over five years
of age should receive an adult's share of rice, but that between the ages of five an ten his share of cloth should be
half that of an adult.   A servant above the age of fifty,
having to support children at home under 16, was to
receive a full share.   One full share of rice was also allowed for each family for the care of its other domestics.

The rules of 1095 provided that a person not resident
within the locality could receive no grants, but one re-
turning home before the fifth day of the month was to
receive his share (1098).   For the support of servants
and slaves, no matter how many there might be in a
family, no more than five shares were to be given; but
bachelors could not claim any shares for servants.

In 1098 the age limit for children was taken away, and
any child, two months after birth, could be registered
together with his mother's name and be counted as a
member of the family.

In 1689 it was provided that children should receive

an adult share only after reaching the age of an adult—
i. e., sixteen. At this age a boy would be brought to
the ancestral temple accompanied by his father, elder
brother, and elders of the immediate family, and there
he would be initiated into full membership in the clan.
This always took place at the spring or autumnal sacrifices.

Special Grants : Certain persons in the clan received
special grants under certain conditions. They were :
students pursuing or preparing for a literary career,
aged persons, and widows.

Young men inclined toward a literary career, and
thus on the road to governmental preferment and Imperial honors, were greatly encouraged in their preparation, because their preferment and honors would reflect
glory upon the clan which produced them.   The rules of
1073 made several provisious for the scholars attending
the Imperial examinations, and those engaged in the
teaching professions. The rules of 1689, amplified these
rules and arranged gifts in grades according to the
literary progress of the scholars. Those who did not
need gifts were permitted to refuse them in favor of
the more needy.

Persons over sixty years of age, according to the
rules of 1689, were given an extra share of support; over
seventy, two extra shares; at eighty, three extra shares;
at ninety, four extra shares; and if without descendants,
an added share. The total number of shares for a person could not exceed five. This provision shows the
reverence for age which is in full accordance with the
mores of patriarchal society.

A widow having passed her third year in widowhood
was registered and received on her own account a full
share of support. At the fifth year of her widowhood

she received an extra share; at the tenth, two extra shares; at the fifteenth, three extra shares; at the twentieth, four extra shares. Beyond this there was no increase. Upon remarriage support was withdrawn.

For special occasions, such as funerals and marriages, families were assisted by the clan estate.

Conclusion : The custom is not uncommon for persons of much wealth to devote their benevolences to their clans, in the distribution of goods or in the founding of useful institutions, such as schools, or in the construction of public works, such as roads and bridges. But an extensive system such as that of the Van Clan is rare. A commoner system is one in which mutual benefit operates more directly. The Clan store consists of voluntary contributions of grain from individual farmers during harvest seasons, and is used for the relief of distress in poor years. Such a system is both prevalent and ancient; Chu-tse, the great editor of the Confucian Classics, was said to have founded one for his home town in 1181 (Sung dynasty).[1]

II. THE VILLAGE COMMUNITY

Local Spirit : We have considered the operation of mutual benefit, based upon the clan, or consanguinity; we will now consider its operation based on local spirit.

We may regard clan consciousness, *i. e.*, consciousness of kind based upon consanguinity, as the simplest expression of what we know as social consciousness in its broadest meaning. It is the simplest because it is elementary and primary; it appeared earliest in social evolution, and has always been an important element in the later development of social consciousness. The next simplest expression of social consciousness is what we may call

[1] *Tö-i-lu,* bk. v, sec. i.

"local spirit" or localism. It is an attachment to a
locality primarily, and secondarily attachment of members of the locality to one another.

We have already referred to the tendency of clans to
localize. But in the complexities of migration localities
become settled by families of more than one clan,
and finally by many families representing many clans,
perhaps with no single clan numerically preponderant.
A fair-sized village is of this description. In such a village community, the members are conscious of an attachment for the place, created and strengthened perhaps
by generations of residence, by associations of childhood,
and by identification of economic interests. The occupation of a common locality becomes a basis upon which
the members build their social intercourse. Solidarity
may be strengthened by intermarriage among the different clans, by division of labor in local industries and by
the recognition of community interests, which are sym-
bolized in the worship of local deities.

The Village Government: The village is a self-govern-
ing group, although it is politically under the district
magistrate, who has jurisdiction over all the villages
within his district. In self-government and in its relation to the political organization of the country, the village has been said to resemble the early New England
communities, with their town-meeting government.[2]
The headmen of the village are elected by the members
of the village, and have delegated powers to control its
affairs and to promote its interests. Their services may
or may not be paid for,[2] and they remain in office during
good behavior. Their public duties consist in the main-

---

[1] Morse, *Trade and Administration of the Chinese Empire*, p. 47.
[2] Williams, *Middle Kingdom*, vol. i, p. 482.

tenance of roads, supervision of fairs, building and up-
keep of public edifices, sinking of wells, engagement of
theatrical companies, policing of the place, *etc.*[1]

In the cultural, economic and industrial life of the village, co-operation is expressed prominently in the conduct of markets and fairs, in the communal "village
hunts," in the associations for the watching and gather-
ing of crops, in the communal education of the young,
and in public maintenance of religious worship and the-
atricals.[2]

Village Charities: For charitable purposes there are
local societies for the care of foundlings, poor families
and their children,[3] mutual loan associations, and mutual
providential associations.

Mutual Loan Societies: Of the reason for the formation of mutual loan societies, Smith says:

Every Chinese has constant occasion to use money in sums
which it is very difficult for him to command. The rate of
interest is always so high that a man who is compelled to
borrow a considerable amount, upon which he must pay interest at two and a half, three, or even four per cent a month,
will not improbably be swamped by the endeavor to keep up
with his creditors. . . . By distributing the payments over a
long period, and by the introduction of an element of friend-
ship into a merely commercial transaction, the Chinese is able
to achieve the happy result of uniting business with pleasure.[4]

Concerning the operation of these mutual loan societies, the following description contains the essential elements:

[1] Smith, *Village Life in China,* p. 227.
[2] Smith, *ibid., passim.*
[3] See Chapter III, Charity.
[4] Smith, *op. cit.,* p. 152.

The simplest of the many plans by which mutual loans are effected is the contribution of a definite sum by each member of the society in rotation to some other one of their number. When all the rest have paid their assessment to the last man on the list, each one will have received back all that he put in, and no more. . . . The man who is in most need of money invites certain of his friends to co-operate with him, and in turn to invite certain of their friends to do the same. When the requisite number has been secured, the members assemble and fix the order in which they each shall have the use of the common fund. This would probably be decided by lot. Unless the amount in question is a very trifling one, every meeting of the members for business purposes will be accompanied by a feast attended by all the partners, and paid for either by the one for whose benefit the association was organized, or by the person whose turn it is to use the common fund.[1]

Various other elements enter into these mutual loan transactions, such as the payment of interest for the use of the common funds; and the size of the membership in the society and the period of its existence are quite variable.

Mutual Providential Associations: Families and individuals of moderate means provide for special drains upon their resources occasioned by such events as weddings and funerals by co-operation. Societies for such purposes follow the model of mutual loan societies, with special memberships, *i. e.*, those who have either the family functions above mentioned on hand, or expect their occurrence in the near future with reasonable certainty.[2]

Mutual providential associations usually operate with the least display of commercialism. The following regulation of a society for funerals is an illustration. It provides for a membership of 32, divided into four depart-

---

[1] Smith, *ibid.,* p. 153.   [2] *Ibid.,* pp. 189-190.

ments, presumably corresponding to the residences of the members, east, west, north and south. Each department has an elected head, through whom business is transacted. In case a death occurs in the home of any member of the society, the four departments contribute money voluntarily and forward it to the bereaved family through the four departmental heads. The family is not expected to make any formal acknowledgment. The members attend the funeral and assist in its arrangements.[1]

III. PROVINCIAL AND DISTRICT CLUBS[2]

The Basis of Association: In large trading cities and towns of China there are always present more or less people from distant cities, who have come for trade, travel, and sometimes for fulfilling official appointments. These people, while mixing freely with the natives of the place, are inclined to segregate into separate groups according to their several provinces or cities. They form what are known as provincial clubs. It is natural for fellow-provincials and fellow-townsmen to feel drawn toward one another while residing among strangers. The attachment with one's native place is not easily dissolved; in fact, it is apt to be strengthened by absence. The custom of reckoning one's birthplace by that of one's grandfather, which obtains in China universally, tends further to prolong the attachment with one's native place. This attachment for a common native place is the ground of association among the co-provincials.

The number of provincial and district clubs in any one city is varied according to the importance of the place as

[1] *Tö-i-lu,* bk. viii, sec. i.
[2] Morse, *Gilds of China,* pp. 35-48.

a trading centre. The city of Shanghai, in the province of Kiangsu, had a Chinese population of 488,000 in 1910, of which 232,982 were natives of 17 outside provinces. One province alone sent out 168,761 individuals, while the smallest number from a single province was 407. There must be therefore as many provincial clubs as there are provinces represented, and probably many more. A much smaller city, Chingkiang, is reported to have at least twelve such clubs,[2] composed of members from eight outside provinces.

Functions of the Clubs: *Social and Charitable*: These district and provincial clubs are called Hwei-Kwan.[3] They exist for mutual protection and aid and social and business intercourse. The membership of a Hwei-kwan consists of all reputable natives of the home province or district. The government of the club is vested in the hands of one or more managers, elected by the members. The income of the club is derived from assessment upon the members, initiation fees and rentals of real estate.

The club naturally serves as an agency for the practice of philanthropy both among its own members and others. It takes care of transients from the home province or district, assists needy members, provides free transportation or burial of poor co-provincials, helps needy students, co-provincials, who come to the place for their Imperial examinations, and helps members in the redress of wrongs. It becomes, moreover, a convenient channel through which members may be reached

[1] Population for the "Port Settlement" only, 1910, in *China Mission Year Book*, 1911.

[2] *Imperial Maritime Customs, Decennial Report*, 1892-1901, vol. i, p. 461.

[3] Morse, *op. cit.*, pp. 35-38.

by appeals for subscription to charitable works of the place where they are.

IV TRADE AND CRAFT GUILDS [1]

The Basis of Association : Association in trade and craft guilds is based upon community of interests, industrial, professional and commercial. The guilds are societies, with specific objects in view, and the consciousness of kind among members is based upon neither considerations of consanguinity nor of locality in itself, although the latter must necessarily affect guild formation, but upon common ecnomic and cultural interests.

The number of guilds is unlimited, for there are possible as many kinds of guilds as there are trades, professions and forms of labor. And so there are bankers' guilds, tea guilds, druggists' guilds, fishmongers' guilds, millers' guilds, wheelbarrow guilds, physicians' guilds, and so on. They are known as Kung-so, or Public Offices.[2]

Functions of the Guilds : Trade and Charity : The guilds exist primarily for the promotion of the interests of the specific trades, crafts, *etc.* They therefore exercise control of the trades, fix wages and prices, regulate supplies of professional services, and exercise other functions pertaining to the interests they represent. The government and support of the guilds follow the general lines described in connection with provincial clubs.

In matters of social relief, these guilds become mutual benefit agencies. Members assist one another and their families in misfortune, their association being the ground for co-operation in relief. Moreover, just as provincial clubs are convenient channels through which to reach their members for subscriptions to charitable

[1] Morse, *ibid.*, pp. 9-34.   [2] Morse, *ibid.*, p. 9.

works, so these craft and trade guilds are equally convenient channels through which to gain the support of shop-keepers, business establishments, professional and labor bodies for charitable works. This method of raising funds is commonly resorted to by philanthropic institutions. It is a fruitful method, as the guilds are able to unite the trades and make them contribute as corporations for such objects. Thus, the Hall of United Benevolence at Shanghai systematically appeals to various guilds for their support. The following is a sample of such an appeal :

At the establishment of the institution in the 9th year of Kiaking, it comprised the four departments of relief of widows, support of the aged, dispensing of coffins and burial of the poor. They were afterwards extended by the support of a free school, a fund for sparing animal life, the supply of water buckets and padded clothes for assisting in case of fire, funeral expenses, the relief of starving strangers, wayside deaths and casualties by drowning, all involving a great expenditure. We have been constantly favored, Worthy Gentlemen, by your donations, annual subscriptions and contributions, besides the voluntary 10 cash coffin-tickets, voluntary vagrant-tickets, and voluntary padded-coat-tickets; you have opened your purses and cheerfully aided the effecting of all those objects. In the first month of the present year our magistrate opened a refuge for the board and lodging of destitute sick and infirm. This necessarily involved us in a large amount of expenditure and the income was not sufficient to meet the outlay. We have been led to consider how that which is raised by many is easily supported, and how the joining of many small pieces will soon make a whole skin. Therefore, as at our instance, the honorable guild of the bean merchants increased their voluntary impost, we respectfully solicit the honorable guilds of the cloth merchants here and in the south of Tsz'-ki in Chekiang to follow the same plan pursued by the bean merchants and to send us in a regular subscription. Thus by the conscientious assistance to so worthy an object it will be perpetuated.[1]

Voluntary Assessment for Charitable Purposes : The guilds have the practice of making assessments upon their members for charitable purposes based upon the volume of business they enjoy. These assessments are arranged by the managers of the guilds and are made known by public proclamations. The following is a sample of such a guild-enactment :[2]

The worthy scholars of Shanghai, in consequence of the subscription purchase of the free burial-ground by Tang, the former magistrate of this city, agreed upon adopting the name of Tung-Jin Tang (United Benevolence Hall), and with noble elevation of mind purchased several halls and rooms for a public place of the institution. At the commencement of the 9th year of Kiaking it was determined to do good by the effecting of four objects. The spirit of United Benevolence is very wide, and it is difficult to say where it should begin and where end. As it is, the support of the aged, relief of widows, with the procuring of coffins and burial are four objects affecting the greatest amount of misery of the living or of the dead, and which are also most striking to the eye and wounding to the heart. It is therefore imperative that with unremitting efforts these should be made their first business. But for such undertakings the necessary expenditure is very large. Benevolent purposes should be universally upheld. We, of this branch of trade, therefore, fearful lest at any time our resources for subscriptions should be limited, conceived that nothing could be better than to subscribe small sums according to the supply of commodity, which would be a plan for the perpetuation of a continual contribution. We, accordingly, came to a public determination that from the middle of the first month of the

[1] *Chinese Repository,* vol. xv, p. 417.

[2] *Ibid.,* vol. xv, pp. 414-415.

present year, with the exception of rice, every description of bean, wheat, pulse, *etc.*, should for every 100 piculs pay a subscription of 14 cash and the bean-cakes 7 cash for every 100 piculs. This subscription is to be paid into the hands of the monthly treasurer, according to the monthly supply of the trade, for the public fund of the Tung-Jin-Tang. There may not be the slightest concealment or diminution which would at once destroy the invariable principle of justice on which we wish to act, and if any discovery of fraud should hereafter take place, it is determined that a heavy fine and forfeiture shall be the penalty.

But as our trade has been gradually flourishing and the objects of the institution demand of us to supply the deficiency from our surplus, and since also the operations of the institution are daily extending, it is our humble opinion that the promotion of good and bestowal of blessing tends to increase the prosperity of our trade.

The enforcement of the enactment by one trade-guild resulted in enlisting 75 stores which were members of the guild to contribute regularly to the charity fund by voluntary assessment. We may therefore regard the guilds as not only promoting the welfare of their own members, but also as being powerful agencies for the support of outside charities.

Conclusion : From the foregoing considerations it appears that the social organization of the Chinese people is such as greatly to facilitate not only the cultivation of co-operation and mutual aid, but also to render easy the application of these principles in the field of practical philanthropy.

CHAPTER V

CIVIC BETTERMENT

Philanthropy as Promotion of Social Welfare: In the foregoing chapters we have described two phases of philanthropy as understood and developed among the Chinese, *viz.*, charity for the dependent classes of society, and mutual benefit. It remains for us to describe the third phase of Philanthropy, namely, Civic Betterment. In including this last phase within the field of philanthropy, we are understanding the term in its broadest significance, that is, Promotion of Social Welfare.

According to Chinese conception and practice, civic betterment is a legitimate department of philanthropy and it is a legitimate field in which one may devote one's altruistic energies. Thus one person may found a free school for the education of youth, another may open his private park to the public, and thus provide general opportunity for esthetic and cultural enjoyment, and a third person may contribute toward building a bridge or maintaining a free ferry service. All would be called philanthropists or social benefactors.

The inaction of the Government toward social welfare has been such that the problem of civic betterment has fallen almost entirely upon the shoulders of the people themselves. To show the attitude of Government toward the social welfare of the people, and the freedom with which the people are allowed to undertake the work by themselves, we will briefly describe the political organization under which the people find themselves both in theory and in practise.

The Chinese Government, in Theory and in Practise: The Imperial Government of the Chinese Empire has been generally known as an Absolute Oriental Monarchy. It is so in theory at least. The Emperor rules by divine right; the people are his subjects. His will is the state; and disobedience is treason. He governs the empire with the assistance of his ministers, who together with other high officials form what is known as the Metropolitan Administration, and with the service of civil and military officials appointed and sent by the throne to their posts throughout the empire. The people are supposed to have no share in the government. But this absolute monarchy is true only in theory. In practise it is far from being absolute. If we study closely the political organization of the country, we find that the Imperial Government has been founded on a principle, more in accord with Spencer's view of minimum state authority than with an imperialist's conception of state authority.

For administration the country is divided into provinces, the provinces divided into prefectures, and the prefectures into districts, which are the smallest administrative units.[1] The districts are governed by magistrates, the magistrates are supervised by prefects, the prefects are under the jurisdiction of the governors of the provinces, and the provinces stand in a relation of quasi-independence to the Central or Metropolitan Administration. The Central Government appoints all the officials of the empire and exercises power of removal of the same, makes laws and levies taxes, and employs

[1] There are 183 prefectures in the 18 provinces of China proper, and 1,443 districts.

the provincial and subordinate officials to enforce the laws and collect the taxes. Beyond these minimum requirements for administrative purposes and a general disciplinary oversight by the Central government, the provinces are left largely to their own control. Hence it has been said, "the government of China is an autocratic rule superposed on a democracy."[1]

The District Municipality: The Imperial Rule comes into contact with the people through the District Magistrate, who is the appointed official and representative of the Government for the smallest political division, the District. His jurisdiction extends over a walled city and the surburban and rural territory lying around it as far as the boundaries of neighboring Districts. The District is the civic, political, judicial and fiscal unit, whereby the people of China are divided. The District is consequently the most important unit of social and political organization, and the Magistrate, the most important Government official so far as the people are concerned.

Paternalism: The District Magistrate is the holder of a very large number of offices and he performs many functions. He is the Mayor of the District, the police Magistrate of the city, the Court of first instance in all civil cases arising in the District, the Registrar of the landed property of the inhabitants, the Tax collector for the Provincial and Metropolitan Administrations, the Poor Relief Commissioner, the Commissioner of Public Works and Buildings, and the Guardian of the Morals and Physical well-being of the people of his jurisdiction. In short he is everything, and so metaphorically is known as the "Father and Mother" of his people.[2]

[1] Morse, *Trade and Administration of Chinese Empire,* p. 46.
[2] Morse, *ibid.,* pp. 69-72.

Defects In Administration: In theory therefore, the social welfare of the people is a well recognized function of the Government and is amply provided for by law. But in practise, there are serious defects in Public Finance and Administrative organization which prevent the District Magistrate from carrying on his functions for social welfare, or oblige him to undertake only an indispensable minimum of the work. These defects are as follows: (1) The District Magistrate has no proper funds at his disposal, specifically designated for his various functions and offices; he must find the funds himself. (2) The Magistrate is given an insignificant official salary, a sum entirely inadequate as compensation for his duties and responsibilities, for maintaining the dignity of his office and for maintaining his subordinates. He is expected to derive his real compensation from emoluments of his office. (3) The chief source for funds to carry on the District Administration is the land-tax. But the Magistrate is also the tax-collector for the Provincial and Metropolitan Administrations. That is to say, the income of the tax is not all retained for local purposes. Out of what may be retained for local purposes, the Magistrate finds the funds for his administration, and the salaries for his subordinates, and for himself. But the tax has been fixed by tradition; and there is no possibility of increase, without antagonizing the people, since in the utilization of the revenue the people have no voice. Under these circumstances, no motive arises to prevent the Magistrate from appropriating as much as possible from the official revenue both for himself, and for his friends in office, or from neglecting the local needs of the people excepting the absolutely unavoidable. Rarely do Magistrates impoverish themselves in order to be the "Father and Mother" of their people.

What is called official corruption in Chinese Government is therefore due not merely to human weakness in the officials but also to defects in the organization of the Government itself. Reform in the organization of the Government is therefore more needed than reform in the individual officials.

State Neglect: The result is a government with a well-meaning paternalism and a theory of existing for the well-being of the people, but in reality impotent to promote their interests, and so estranged from their sympathies. The District municipality becomes like the other political divisions of the country merely an administrative unit of the Central Government, and not an organ for the satisfaction of local needs of the people, as it should be. The hundred and one undertakings, such as roads, street-lights, removal of rubbish, water-supply, school system, police, fire-protection, *etc.*, which people of the West are accustomed to regard as functions of a municipal government are, with a few exceptions of recent date, never undertaken by the proper Government officials. For these, the people are left to work out their own salvation in perfect freedom. Thus, the Government of China as far as the well-being of the people is concerned resembles a temporarily set-up tent, fastened to the national soil with a few pegs and propped up with a few poles here and there, rather than a permanent building of stone and mortar firmly grounded on national foundations.

Practical Democracy: One condition which has made the people tolerate a government estranged from their lives is its permitting them to live in perfect freedom and autonomy, provided the minimum taxation is paid and the moral principles of the Penal Code are observed. What the people everywhere desire is unhampered freedom for pursuing their livelihood, and this the Chinese have in abundance. A keen American observer, Hon. Holcombe, writes thus :

In point of fact the Chinese are governed less than almost any nation in the world. So long as they pay their taxes and violate none of the requirements of the moral code, they are not disturbed by the authorities. A thousand and one official inspections, exactions and interferences, common enough everywhere in America and Europe are quite unknown in China.[1]

Dr. Coolidge, author of *Chinese Immigration*, says: " If the Chinese Government be regarded from the top it appears to be a centralized autocracy; if from the bottom, a pure democracy."

Popular Co-operative Undertakings: The government's neglect is the people's opportunity. We have shown the relative part taken by the Government and the people respectively in charities : that the Governmnnt takes a relatively insignificant part in the relief of the dependent classes, and that the people have the work almost entirely in their own hands. We have also shown how the factor of mutual aid among the people enters into the whole fabric of social organization. We will now show how, in the absence of an aggressive Governmental pursuit of social welfare, the people themselves have undertaken the necessary philanthropic work by co-operative measures grouped under the title of Civic Betterment.

I. FREE EDUCATIONAL OPPORTUNITIES

Government Education : Until the institution of Hioh Pu, or Board of Education by the Metropolitan Admin-

[1] *Real Chinese Question*, p. 4.

istration in 1903, there was no national system of education.   Prior to that date, there had existed for upwards
of ten centuries the Imperial Literary Examinations.
But these were concerned more with tests for civil service, rather than with the actual education of the people.
The latter has almost entirely been in the hands of the
people themselves.   Since the institution of the Educational Board, the Government has inauguarated a system
of public education which intends eventually to cover the
empire with free educational opportunities as completely
as in any modern country.   In 1910 there were already
42,650 new educational institutions of all grades in China;
but it is a note-worthy fact that the public and private
institutions out-numbered Government institutions.[1]

Free Charity Schools: Charity organizations have entered into the field of providing free educational opportunities for the poor.   The Hall of United Benevolence
reported maintaining a free school;[2] and the Hall of
Sustaining Love at Canton reported the maintenance during 1872 of 19 schools with twenty teachers, and 15
schools with 16 teachers in 1873.[3]   We have already
referred to school work for children of widows, and
provision by clans for the education of their own young
people.

Public Lectures: Another instrument for popular education is free lectures.   The reports of the Hall of
Sustaining Love showed that in 1872, the society engaged the services of three lecturers, for a total of 16
months.   In 1873, it engaged three lecturers for a total
of 18 months.[4]   There are also voluntary societies which

---

[1] *China Mission Year Book,* 1911, p. 79.

[2] Report in *Chinese Repository,* vol. xv, pp. 402 *et seq.*

[3] *China Review,* vol. iii, pp. 108 *et seq.*

[4] *China Review,* vol. iii, pp. 108 *et seq.*

take up the work of lecturing.   *Tö-i-lu* contains the
record of a society founded in 1755, which besides distributing books, posters, songs and pictures, conducted
lectures. The method was to have a lecturing team
consisting of earnest and eloquent speakers spend the
first three days of a month at the club house, and then
spend the other seven of the first ten days in the month
in visiting different sections of the city.

The lectures are almost always concerned with morals,
it being the belief that the morals of the people are the
foundation of national prosperity. The following sample
is on record in *Tö-i-lu*[1] :

This society teaches men to be good. Those who come to
hear must have the elements of good already in them. They
have the good intention to come and so they will have good
words to hear. One good word stimulates one good thought,
and the man is good for life: do not depreciate this sentence.
In this way daily dangers may be turned into advantage, and
death itself into life.

Everyone has parents: let him serve them;
Everyone has elders: let him respect them;
Everyone has nighbors: let him be at peace with them;
Everyone has children: let him teach them properly;

Let everyone do his duty: If he does it not, but what he
ought not to do, he becomes a criminal. Note how criminals
are invariably discovered and brought to justice. See what
miserable end do the squanderer and the gambler always come
to. When they founder in trouble, then they envy the lot of
the common laborer who toils in the street earning his honest
livelihood with diligence and in freedom. The good people
are always honored by their neighbors, and prized by their
parents and elders, and blessed by Heaven with prosperous
and numerous progeny. They shed honor upon the name of

[1] Bk. i, sec. ii, p. 19.

their parents and ancestors. This is true filial piety and worthier than sacrifices. Let everyone who hears start the day with a good thought. Those who have been already good, be steadfast; those who are not good, repent; it is never too late to reform.

Literary Censorship: Another function along educational lines is the suppression of indecent literature and a censorship of popular plays and songs. This is generally undertaken by reputable publishers who agree to buy up the indecent literature and destroy their plates. The movement is enforced with fines for recalcitrant publishers.[1]

Other activities, along educational lines, are distribution of tracts, useful information, songs, pictures and posters calculated to improve public morals; and the collection and burning of waste printed matter to inculcate respect for letters. In some cities there are owners of private parks equipped with libraries, zoological sections and aquariums, who open them for the enjoyment of the public, admission being either free or by payment of a nominal fee.

II. PUBLIC SAFETY AND PROTECTION

Under this heading there are several forms of activity engaged in by charity societies and voluntary associations, such as life-saving on water, pilot-boats and fire protection. They are agencies for safety and protection of lives and property.

The Life-saving Station at Wuhu:[2] This association came into existence before the Tai-ping rebellion, *i. e.*, before the middle of the nineteenth century. It has its

[1] Nevius, *China and the Chinese,* p. 221.

[2] Report of the Association in *China Review,* vol. vi, p. 277, *et seq.*

offices along the shore, and its object is to render assistance to persons and boats in distress on the river. Its
equipment consists of life-boats, administration offices,
rooms for the rescued persons and burial ground for the
drowned.

Life-boats : The boats are manned by crews that live
on board all the time. Each boat has a helmsman and
four sailors. On account of the importance of their
duties the crews are carefully selected and disciplined.
The regulations read in part :

Men wishing to serve in the life-boats should come to this
office with their securities when an agreement will be made out
and signed. The Association will not be responsible for
accidents met with in their service, such as slipping overboard
or being lost in stormy weather. All it can do in such cases
is to provide a coffin; it will not listen to claims for compensation.

The crews are required to live on board the boats, and
may not absent themselves without leave. Should any
be called away on account of urgent business, he must
find his own substitute. Gambling, drinking and opium-
smoking are forbidden; criminals may not be sheltered
on board nor contraband goods received thereon. For
light offenses, dismissal from employment is the punishment, but for heavy offenses the offender is handed
over to the penal authorities for punishment.

The boats must always be in readiness. Whether in
day or in night, in storm or in rain, the boats must
put out to render assistance to boats or persons in distress, at the summons of the alarm-drum. For the
encouragement of the crew, they are, besides their
regular wages, rewarded for their diligence. For saving
one life the reward is 1000 coins ; for a corpse recovered

the reward is 500 coins; and during nights the sums are doubled.

In case of an accident, human life must receive first attention, and only after all possible help has been given for rescue of life may attention be turned to the recovery of lost goods. The life-boats must proceed to save life, and after having ascertained that everybody on board the wrecked vessel is accounted for, convey the rescued persons to the station. Should there be anyone missing, search must be made on all sides, and dead or alive every individual must be found before the cargo is attended to.

When a person is saved, he is brought to the office and lodged in the rooms prepared for such transients for three days, during which time he is cared for and clothed by the Association. In the case of a woman refugee, the local constable is notified and he must find her suitable lodging with some married woman of elderly years. With a man, no matter how distant his destination may be, traveling expenses are given him and he is sent away after the third day. But a woman is not sent away until her relatives come to claim her, or at least until her family is notified of the fact.

Careful records of the persons saved, together with their names, home addresses, and the dates are kept at the office. Unclaimed bodies of the drowned are buried by the association. In one year (1876) 52 lives were rescued and 46 corpses recovered on the river. Assistance was given also to many vessels in hardship. Goods recovered are brought to the administration office, where they await reclaiming by the proper owners.

Management and Finances: Association business is taken care of by a salaried Committee of 12 men, who occupy the offices in groups of four at a time. As to the duties of the Committee-men, it is required that they shall always keep in touch with one another, and co-operate heartily, for "it is by co-operation that the good cause can be best furthered."

The finances of the association are derived from several sources. A part of the funds comes from civil officials, but the major part from voluntary contributions. Publicity is rigidly maintained through monthly and annual reports. Of the annual reports, it is recorded, one copy is kept at the association office, another copy goes to the District magistrate, and a third is solemnly burned before the local god.

At this religious performance, all the officers of the Association must be present, and together they make the following declaration:

We, the managers of the Life Saving Association venture to come before thee, O God, and humbly represent that owing to the vastness of the waters and the raging of the billows in the rivers of Wuhu, a sudden squall striking the passing craft and taking the sailors unawares will cause ship-wreck and loss of life.

Though we are aware that the term of a man's life is already decreed and that Heaven's power may not be opposed, yet such sights grieve the heart. Thus it is that we have sought means to save life, and that persons have come together to form a Life Saving association, supported entirely by voluntary contributions. Premises have been erected and boats built with the object of affording security from danger, ensuring a safe passage in stormy weather. A public cemetery has been opened for the burial of the dead and coffins are kept ready for use. Thus are good deeds done, afloat and ashore. A statement of receipts and disbursements has been prepared and in this work of humanity we have been faithful to the trust reposed in us by the benevolent subscribers.

We pray Thee to examine our conduct, and to mete out

justice to us. May we be punished if we have sacrificed the public good to our private ends, and if we have been laborers unworthy of our hire, if we misappropriated public funds, or if we have caused subscribers to fall off by spreading false reports. While on the other hand, may we be recompensed if we have discharged our duty with all fidelity sparing neither trouble nor fatigue. This we pray to the end that good deeds may endure forever. Humbly we submit our statement of accounts for the year now ended.[1]

Public declaration before the gods is obviously prompted by a utilitarian motive: to gain the confidence of the people and to satisfy the supporters of the honesty of the administration. The utilization of the religious propensities of the people may not be disadvantageous in winning support for charitable undertakings, and we find many a charitable institution having patronage deities and religious observances.

Other riparian cities have similar life-boats, such as Ching-Kiang, Nanking, and Ichang. The boats of the last city are known as Red-boats on account of the color of their paint. Here the boats were first managed by a co-operative society, but later were taken over by the Government because of the importance of the service to the trade of the place.

The " Red-Boats" of Ichang :[2] Ichang is a city situated at a place along the Yantse River, where the stream enters a ravine between high mountainous shores and where there are treacherous rapids. Before the establishment of the Red-boats Service, the dangers of the river, although known, were avoided with difficulty, much loss of lives and property often occurring. At first the

[1] *China Review,* vol. vi, p. 283.

[2] *Imperial Maritime Customs, Decennial Report,* 1892-1901, vol. i, pp. 201-204.

fishing boats in the neighborhood were paid small sums to enlist them in the work of rescue. But the plan did not succeed, because it often happened that at the time of a wreck no fishing boat was near enough to the scene of disaster to render any assistance. In 1854 a prosperous merchant, by name Li Yun-kuei, collected subscriptions from the traders whose junks passed through the rapids, and with the money thus raised he built three boats after the pattern of the fishing boats, but distinguished from the latter by being painted red, to be engaged exclusively in the life-saving and piloting work. The society formed to manage the boats was called K'ang Chi T'ang. Later the number of boats was increased to 27. The Government, recognizing the value of the service, subsidized it, and finally caused it to be transformed into a Government service and it has since been managed by the Government with special officials in charge.

Fire Protection : Chinese municipalities do not have fire departments, and so for protection against fires, the people must band themselves together in co-operative associations. These associations usually conform to the streets or wards into which a city is divided. The result is a net-work of fire brigades and stations covering the whole city. In some places the administration of these brigades is taken care of by the charity societies. Thus the Hall of United Benevolence at Shanghai has a fire protection department.[1] It maintains eleven stations throughout the city. Each station is provided with equipment for fighting fires, such as engines, lanterns, firemen's uniforms, *etc.* Each station has ten men under a headman. These men are paid for their services after each occurrence of fire.

[1] *Chinese Repository*, vol. xv, pp. 409-410.

III. FREE PUBLIC SERVICE

In free public service we include not only agencies of transportation, such as ferries, but also means of communication, such as roads and bridges, maintained by voluntary subscription to serve a public free of charge or for a nominal fee. Thus it has been observed by foreign travelers in China:

It is also worthy of remark that most of the roads and fine archbridges, as well as the public buildings of China, are constructed by voluntary donations. In connection with these public works, it is very common to see stone tablets erected, containing the names of the donors and the amounts of their subscriptions.[1]

Such undertakings are usually entrusted to local charity societies and sometimes to special societies.

Lights and Bridges : The Hall of United Benevolence maintains lights at four places along water-ways around Shanghai, and pays for the services of four men engaged in taking care of the lights. It repairs roads and pavements, cleans sewers, and keeps up the bridges. During 1909, besides miscellaneous repairing, it paid for 574 yards of road-paving, replaced a bridge-railing, and repaired eight bridges.[2]

Free Ferry Service : The Life Saving Association at Wuhu ran a free ferry across the river, according to its report[3] for 1875. It possessed six boats for this service, two having a capacity of 60 passengers each, two forty passengers each, and two ten each. The boats were manned according to their sizes. For the large ones,

[1] J. L. Nevius, *China and the Chinese*, p. 224.
[2] Report of the Hall for 1909.
[3] *China Review*, vol. vi, pp. 277-283.

there was a helmsman and four sailors; for the middle-sized, a helmsman and three sailors, and for the small ones, a helmsman and two sailors.

On both sides of the river there were landing stations and ticket offices. A flag raised upon a pole indicated the period during which the service was in operation. It was limited to the day-time. In the night and in severe storms, the boats would not run and the flag was not hoisted up.

Each passenger went aboard with a ticket. When the full number of tickets was collected, the boat proceeded for the other shore. But for special parties, such as a funeral party, a physician in his professional visitation, a marriage party, the boats would cross the river without the full number.

These boats were maintained by voluntary subscriptions. As an inducement, a subscriber for a certain sum of money would be given a ferry pass, if he had use for one, which entitled the holder to prompt service.

IV. Municipal Self-government by the People

Its Evolution: The work of the philanthropic and co-operative associations for civic betterment, as described above, belongs to the class of municipal functions and has been undertaken by the people themselves because of neglect by the Government authorities, as we have already pointed out. Beginning in voluntary co-operation for mutual benefit, these undertakings gradually become established by custom and finally are recognized as public institutions, both by the people and the civil authorities. At first scattered and uncoördinated, the agencies for these undertakings gradually coalesce and consolidate into one system. Thus results what is virtually municipal self-government by the people.

Instead of the civil authorities protesting against the encroachment on their authorities, they encourage this development of popular self-rule by giving it full recognition and freedom of action.

The Case of the Newchwang Guild: An early case illustrating this evolution is that of the Local Guild of Newchwang, Manchuria, recorded in the *Decennial Report of Imperial Maritime Customs* for 1882–1891.[1] The Local Guild is made up of the principal native merchants of the city, and practically combines in itself the duties of a municipal council and those of a chamber of commerce. It maintains order in the streets, takes care of the roads, drains and reservoirs, controls public lands, administers poor relief, subsidizes charitable institutions, controls banks, regulates exchanges of trade, marts and transportation. It finances its activities by taxation upon transactions between merchants not natives of the city but residing and doing business therein, by collecting bridge-dues upon carts transporting goods, and shop dues; for all of which the guild has the authorization of the local civil officials. The authority of the guild and its method of administration is shown in the proclamations it issues. The following is one concerning bridge-dues :

It is generally understood that living traffic is a sure sign of a town's prosperity. To encourage traffic, therefore the public thorough-fares must be kept in good repair.

A former president of the Guild built bridges across the streams and tidal creeks in the vicinity of Ying-tsu for public use, but as nothing was done to keep them in repair, the strong current gradually undermined the supports, so that many bridges were in danger of collapsing.

[1] Pp. 34 *et seq.*

The roads, too were the cause of universal complaint.

A subscription was consequently raised from the resident merchants to defray the annual outlay for repairing the roads and bridges in the neighborhood of the port.

During the Summer of the second year of Emperor Kuang Hsu (1876) continued rains did much harm to the public thoroughfares, suspending thereby a great deal of the cart traffic. This state of affairs coming to the ears of the Taotai, he issued orders to the Guild that the roads and bridges were to be promptly put in thorough repair. This was done at great expense, and the ordinary subscription not proving sufficient to meet the unusual outlay, a plan was devised to tax all carts carrying merchandise. Permission having been received from the Tartar General and the Civil Governor at Moukden, through the influence of the Taotai, a tax was then instituted, which has been continued up to the present time.

The Guild now informs the public that beginning with to-day, the First of the Ninth Moon and ending with the First of the Third Moon of the following year, bridge-dues will be levied on all carts laden with produce of any kind at the following rates: [1]

Local Self-Government, A Growing Movement: During recent years, local self-government by the people is developing in many cities and towns. It is distinctly encouraged by the Imperial Government as a step in the preparation toward Constitutional Parliamentary Government. A short time ago the writer sent out some questions to his friends at Shanghai in regard to municipal self-government in that city. The replies are significant. They show that self-government is directly sanctioned by the local civil officials and indirectly by the Imperial Government; that local government is in the hands of the franchised citizens of the city, who elect the officers of the

[1] *Ibid.,* p. 37.

local administration, but that the district magistrate acts as a director and advisor and that it practically takes over all the functions of a municipality, including the powers of taxation and police. The new local self-government supervises the educational institutions, opens free schools, undertakes sanitation, street-cleaning, public works, lighting, police, traffic regulation, supervision of commercial amusements, inspection of food-markets; it makes its own laws and enforces them, and collects taxes. The taxes are called Public Welfare Taxes, and consist of house and shop tax, license of vehicles and of boats, tax on advertisement spaces, commercial amusements, and food-markets. An interesting fact is that the budgets of the Shanghai Municipal Self-government contain an estimate of the yearly incomes and expenditure of the charitable institutions of the city, indicating that the municipality is aiming at including among its functions supervision and support of these hitherto voluntary and independent institutions. The new self-government administration does not displace the old civil government of the city. That is to say, the magistrate who is the appointed representative and agent of the provincial and imperial administrations still retains his office, collects the land taxes and forwards them to the higher administrations. There is a division of labor. The magistrate takes care of the city as far as it is an administrative unit of the empire; while the new local government takes care of the city as such for the satisfaction of its local needs.

The New Political Régime : In the famous constitution of 1908 promulgated by the Imperial Government, local self-government is fully instituted and defined. In principle it aims to preserve the functions and powers which the district magistrate now exercises intact, and to superadd upon the existing régime, the new organization for local self-government, along the lines we have already described in connection with the local self-government of Shanghai city.

It is thus apparent that by successive and almost imperceptible gradations, what was, in the beginning, mere voluntary co-operative measures on the part of the people for mutual protection and civic betterment on the occasion of official omission in a political organization, wherein popular franchise was unknown, has become one of the fundamental features of a new order of political life, wherein popular franchise and self-government are the essential features. The outward suddenness, apparently suggested by the promulgation of the new Constitution and the transition from an Absolute Monarchy to a democratic form of government is therefore more apparent than real. Silent causes have been working for generations under the shadow of the old régime, and the new régime is their natural consummation.

CHAPTER VI

Conclusion: Rise of National Self-consciousness and Solidarity

Chinese Philanthropy, the Product of National Genius : Chinese Philanthropy is a product of the genius of the Chinese Nation. It is organically related with the life, tradition and ideals of the nation, and from them has derived its energy, its guiding principles and characteristics. It is an expression of Chinese civilization.

Democratic Foundation : The notable characteristic of Chinese Philanthropy is its democratic foundation. Instead of being a state institution, it has been more a popular one ; instead of being fostered under the paternalism and direction of the state, it has been developed by the co-operation and initative of the people.

Esprit de Corps of Minor Social Groups : The spirit of Chinese Philanthropy indicates a developed social consciousness in the hearts of the people. There is a strong sense of social solidarity, which shows itself in the many sharing the burden of the poverty, want and misfortune of the few, in the readiness to give mutual aid, and in the voluntary co-operative undertaking for civic betterment. The sense of social solidarity is strongest in the *esprit de corps* of the minor social groups within the nation, such as the clan, the village, the District, the Province, and the guilds.

Absence of National Consciousness in the Past : Until the beginning of the present century, there had not been a national self-consciousness and solidarity comparable in strength with the spirit and solidarity of the minor social groups. This is attributable both to the presence of unfavorable conditions, and to the absence of favorable conditions for the development and sustenance of the spirit of nationalism. The gigantic territory of the empire, the want of convenient and rapid means of communication between widely-separated parts, the resulting effect in the diversification of local dialects, and to a less extent of local customs, and the absence of a powerful, aggressive, centralized national Government have been some of the conditions which deterred the rise of national consciousness and solidarity in the people.

Geographical Isolation and Absence of Conflict : But there was a condition, whose presence in the national experience of China exercised an even greater influence than the above-mentioned conditions in the determent of the rise of national consciousness and solidarity, namely, geographical isolation. During historic times since the occupation of the empire in its present dimensions in the second century B. C. and until the last century A. D., China was practically cut off from intercourse with the other historic peoples of the world by physical barriers, the oceans and the mountains. The only important people with whom China came into hostile contact for any considerable number of times during the 2000 years down to the middle of the nineteenth century were the Tartars from the north and northwest. Geographical isolation has meant, therefore, absence of international conflict. History seems to show that conflict between nations is the chief, potent condition for the rise of national consciousness and solidarity.

Governmental Decentralization : The absence of international conflict also furnishes a reason for the non-appearance of a powerful, aggressive, centralized national government. So long as China remained an isolated country, having enough productive land and possessions to satisfy its political ambitions, and having the natural physical barriers to protect it from foreign attack, it did not need a very strong, aggressive and centralized national government. There was need only for so much of organized government as would insure the primary conditions of social well-being within the realm, such as peace, order, security of property, safety of life, and freedom for lawful pursuit of livelihood. For the assurance of these primary conditions of social well-being, decentralization of government may be just as favorable a policy as centralization, and moral authority may be more successful than authority of force, if socialization is sufficiently advanced and the social population sufficiently homogeneous. Decentralization and moral authority would be preferred both for their economy and their compatibility with the purpose of organized government in such a country. The final picture of the country would be something as follows: the country would be divided into administrative units, such as provinces, prefects and districts; each political division would be held responsible to the next higher division for the fulfilment of certain administrative duties, but otherwise It would be semi-independent; the central government would be an organ for balancing the works of the various political units, rather than be their taskmaster; the laws of the land would be little more than the crystallization of the customs of the nation; the people would be given great freedom and opportunities of self-government; the government would utilize some popular national ethical system or religion as the means of ruling the people and keeping them in their legitimate spheres of life and activity.

Such has been actually the case with China until recently. Mayers, writing in 1878 says, "the central government of China, so far as a system of this nature is recognized in the existing institutions, is arranged with the object rather of registering and checking the action of the various provincial administrations, than that of assuming a direct initiative in the conduct of affairs." [1] As to the practical freedom and democracy of the Chinese nation, we have already indicated it in Chapter V.

The New National Consciousness and Solidarity: International Relationships: But since the beginning of the 19th century, the conditions of the national life of China have undergone great change. Geographical isolation has disappeared on the advent of ocean steamers; China has become part of the world system of commerce and international relationships; she has measured strength with other peoples, and has compared her civilization with theirs; and so through these international, inter-racial and inter-cultural contacts, the Chinese nation has attained self-consciousness, and the national government is being consolidated and centralized. Thus Morse says: "The hammering of twenty years has welded the Empire together, and the Imperial Government was compelled, in its foreign relationships, to act as a ruler and not as a mere supervisor, and to adopt a more centralized policy." [2]

Improved Internal Communication: Besides, new means of communication have been introduced into the country, such as railroads, steamships, and the telegraph; and the distant parts of the empire are brought closer

[1] Morse, *Trade and Administration of the Chinese Empire,* p. 53.
[2] *Ibid.,* p. 55.

to one another and to the national center, the Capital; and so there is better intercourse and intelligence among the people in the different provinces and districts. Again quoting Morse:

In the old days, too, the communication was slow, and two or three months might elapse before the authorities at Canton could receive a reply to their request for instructions, with the result that much must be left to the man on the spot. The introduction of steamers brought Canton, Nanking and Hankow, the seats of the most important viceroyalties, within a week of the Capital; and the extension of the telegraphs which directly resulted from the Russian difficulty of 1880, brought the most remote of the high provincial authorities into immediate touch with the central administration, and furthered the centralization which had already become established; and now the Empire is ruled from Pekin to an extent unknown while China still played the hermit.[1]

The New Education: There is yet another factor, which is directly fostering the growth of the spirit of nationalism. Speaking of this new factor, as awakening the people to a sense of their citizenship in the nation, Professor Bevan says:

There are two forces that are welding the Chinese people and their government into a single nation, one from without and one from within. Contact with foreign nations has compelled the Chinese nation to assert itself as the actual governing power throughout the whole empire. Increase of knowledge and the birth of a new education have brought the people to a real and truer self-realization; and this realization of self is driving the people to demand a civilization similar to the civilizations which they have discovered around

[1] Morse, *op. cit.*, p. 56.

them. On the one side, there is a movement in the direction of strengthening the central authority and drawing closer the ties between the central administration and the administrations of the constituent parts of the empire, while on the other side there is a demand that the people shall have a share in the making of the laws and in their carrying out when made. The central power is attempting to govern either immediately by itself, or indirectly through its agents more directly and more closely responsible to itself. The people is trying to make its voice heard in the government councils; they are making a distinct attempt to obtain for themselves a share in the legislative and administrative functions of the empire. The Constitution is an effort to combine these two forces. [1]

The Nation-Wide Basis of Philanthropy : With the rise of national self-consciousness and solidarity, philanthropy will acquire a nation-wide basis of operation. On the one hand, the extension of social consciousness throughout the whole nation, uniting the people in all parts of the empire will extend the field of philanthropy, and facilitate its application; on the other hand, the centralization of the Government, the assumption of definite responsibilities and powers by it will ultimately mean a more active participation of the Government in social welfare. Already we find the people of all sections of the country responding to appeals for aid of some particular section in times of misfortune with greater readiness than was obtainable ten or twenty years ago. Already, we see the Government taking up the problem of public education, and initiating other reforms. Furthermore, whereas there was estrangement between the Government and

[1] "The New Chinese Constitution," in *China Mission Year Book*, 1911.

the people formerly, there seems to be a conscious co-operation between the two now, such as has been shown in the co-operation for public education and for the suppression of opium, because it has been for the first time clearly realized that the Government and the people have identical and not variant interests. In other words, the Government is logically bound to assert itself in the promotion of the social welfare of the nation. But in so doing, it will not be so unwise as to discourage the people's activities along the same lines. Rather the Government will co-operate with the people by undertaking those works which lie beyond the power of private voluntary institutions and associations, or beyond that of particular cities, and localities, because of juristic and financial conditions, and by further developing existing undertakings of the people through financial assistance and legislative standardization. This seems to be the new ideal that is actuating the conscience of the people and the government to-day.

A New National Personality : And so a new era in China's life has begun. The social consciousness which was in the past confined within the limits of minor social groups and associations and political divisions has broken forth and merged into the larger consciousness of the nation. The loyalty which people in the past gave unconditionally to their immediate clans, localities, guilds, and provinces, has now found its proper subordination in the new alignment of allegiance to the nation. In this transition from the old to the new era, there is, therefore, a readaptation of the habits of mutual aid and co-operation, trained in the social functioning and experiences of smaller associations, for the functioning and experiences of the larger association, the nation. As a historical fact, and not as a mere figure of speech, the Twentieth Century B. C. witnessed the birth of the Ancient China, and the Twentieth Century A. D. is witnessing the birth of the New China,—the evolution of a new National Personality through new national experiences.

BIBLIOGRAPHY

A partial list of publications cited

L. R. O. Bevan. Article: "The New Chinese Constitution," in *China Mission Year Book*. Shanghai, 1911.

H. C. Chen. *Economic Principles of Confucius and His School.* N. Y., 1911.

China Review. Vols. II, III, VI. Shanghai, 1873-1875, 1877-1878.

Chinese Repository. Vols. XIV, XV, XVI, XVII. Canton, 1845-1848.

Chuang Tzŭ, Mystic, Moralist and Social Reformer. Tr. H. A. Giles. London, 1889.

Decennial Reports, 1882-1892; 1892-1901. *China, Imperial Maritime Customs.* Shanghai.

E. T. Devine. *Principles of Relief.* N. Y., 1904.

F. H. Giddings. *Principles of Sociology.* N. Y., 1896.

J. H. Grey. *Walks in the City of Canton.* 1875.

A. E. Hecker. *A Short History of Women's Rights.* N. Y., 1910.

Hsin Tzŭ. *Essay on Human Nature.*

E. Huntington. *Pulse of Asia.* Boston and N. Y., 1907.

F. H. King. *Farmers of Forty Centuries.* Madison, Wis, 1911.

E. Legouvé. *Moral History of Women.* Tr. from 5th Paris Ed. by J. W. Palmer. N. Y., 1860.

Lî Kî. Collection of Treatises on the Rules of Propriety or Ceremonial Usages. Tr. J. Legge, in *"Texts of Confucianism," Sacred Books of the East,* ed. F. Max Müller. Vols. XXVII, XXVIII. Oxford, 1885.

Liu Hsian. *Lives of Virtuous Women.*

Mencius. Tr. J. Legge, in *Chinese Classics.* 2nd Ed. Rev. Vol. II. Oxford, 1895.

S. Merwins. *Drugging a Nation.* N. Y., 1908.

H. B. Morse. *Gilds of China.* N. Y., 1909.

—— *Trade and Administration of the Chinese Empire.* London, 1908.

J. L. Nevius. *China and the Chinese.* N. Y., 1869.

E. H. Parker. *China, Her History, Diplomacy and Commerce.* London, 1901.

—— *China, Past and Present.* London, 1903.

—— *Studies in Chinese Religion.* N. Y., 1910.

E. A. Ross. *Changing Chinese.* N. Y., 1911.

A. H. Smith. *Village Life in China. A Study in Sociology.* N. Y., 1899.

H. Spencer. *Principles of Biology.*

—— *Principles of Ethics.* N. Y., 1904.

Ta Tsing Leu Lee, Being the Fundamental Laws and a Selection from the Supplementary Statutes of the Penal Code of China. Tr. G. T. Staunton. London, 1810.

Tö-i-lu. Rules and Regulations of Benevolent Institutions. Wu-si, 1869.

Studies in History, Economics and Public Law

Edited by the

Faculty of Political Science of Columbia University

VOLUME XXII, 1905. 520 pp. Price, cloth, $3.50; paper covers, $3.00.

The Historical Development of the Poor Law of Connecticut.
By EDWARD W. CAPEN, Ph.D.

VOLUME XXIII, 1905. 594 pp. Price, cloth, $4.00.

1. The Economics of Land Tenure in Georgia.
By ENOCH MARVIN BANKS, Ph.D.   Price, $1.00.

2. Mistake in Contract. A Study in Comparative Jurisprudence.
By EDWIN C. McKEAG, Ph.D.   Price, $1.00.

3. Combination in the Mining Industry.   By HENRY R. MUSSEY, Ph.D.   Price, $1.00.

4. The English Craft Guilds and the Government.
By STELLA KRAMER, Ph.D.   Price, $1.00.

VOLUME XXIV, 1905. 521 pp. Price, cloth, $4.00.

1. The Place of Magic in the Intellectual History of Europe.
By LYNN THORNDIKE, Ph.D.   Price, $1.00.

2. The Ecclesiastical Edicts of the Theodosian Code.
By WILLIAM K. BOYD, Ph.D.   Price, $1.00.

3. *The International Position of Japan as a Great Power.
By SEIJI G. HISHIDA, Ph.D.   Price, $2.00.

VOLUME XXV, 1906-07. 600 pp. (Sold only in Sets.)

1. *Municipal Control of Public Utilities. By O. L. POND, Ph.D. (Not sold separately.)

2. The Budget in the American Commonwealths.
By EUGENE E. AGGER, Ph.D.   Price, $1.50.

3. The Finances of Cleveland.   By CHARLES C. WILLIAMSON, Ph.D.   Price, $2.00.

VOLUME XXVI, 1907. 559 pp. Price, cloth, $4.00.

1. Trade and Currency in Early Oregon.   By JAMES H. GILBERT, Ph.D.   Price, $1.00.

2. Luther's Table Talk.   By PRESERVED SMITH, Ph.D.   Price, $1.00.

3. The Tobacco Industry in the United States.
By MEYER JACOBSTEIN, Ph.D.   Price, $1.50.

4. Social Democracy and Population.   By ALVAN A. TENNEY, Ph.D.   Price, 75 cents.

VOLUME XXVII, 1907. 578 pp. Price, cloth, $4.00.

1. The Economic Policy of Robert Walpole.   By NORRIS A. BRISCO, Ph.D.   Price, $1.50.

2. The United States Steel Corporation.   By ABRAHAM BERGLUND, Ph.D.   Price, $1.50.

3. The Taxation of Corporations in Massachusetts.
By HARRY G. FRIEDMAN, Ph.D.   Price, $1.50.

VOLUME XXVIII, 1907. 564 pp. Price, cloth, $4.00.

1. DeWitt Clinton and the Origin of the Spoils System in New York.
By HOWARD LEE McBAIN, Ph. D.   Price, $1.50.

2. The Development of the Legislature of Colonial Virginia.
By ELMER I. MILLER, Ph.D.   Price, $1.50.

3. The Distribution of Ownership.   By JOSEPH HARDING UNDERWOOD, Ph.D.   Price, $1.50.

VOLUME XXIX, 1908. 703 pp. Price, cloth, $4.50.

1. Early New England Towns.   By ANNE BUSH MacLEAR, Ph.D.   Price, $1.50.

2. New Hampshire as a Royal Province.   By WILLIAM H. FRY, Ph.D.   Price, $3.00.

VOLUME XXX, 1908. 712 pp. Price, cloth, $4.50; paper covers, $4.00.

The Province of New Jersey, 1664—1738.   By EDWIN P. TANNER, Ph.D.

VOLUME XXXI, 1908. 575 pp. Price, cloth, $4.00.

1. Private Freight Cars and American Railroads.
By L. D. H. WELD, Ph.D.   Price, $1.50.

2. Ohio before 1850.   By ROBERT E. CHADDOCK, Ph.D.   Price, $1.50.

3. Consanguineous Marriages in the American Population.
By GEORGE B. LOUIS ARNER, Ph.D.   Price, 75 cents.

4. Adolphe Quetelet as Statistician.   By FRANK H. HANKINS, Ph.D.   Price, $1.25.

VOLUME XXXII, 1908. 705 pp. Price, cloth, $4.50; paper covers, $4.00.

The Enforcement of the Statutes of Laborers.   By BERTHA HAVEN PUTNAM, Ph.D.

VOLUME XXXIII, 1908-1909. 635 pp. Price, cloth, $4.50.

1. Factory Legislation in Maine.   By E. STAGG WHITIN, A.B.   Price, $1.00.

2. *Psychological Interpretations of Society.
By MICHAEL M. DAVIS, JR., Ph.D.   Price, $2.00.

3. *An Introduction to the Sources relating to the Germanic Invasions.
By CARLTON HUNTLEY HAYES, Ph.D.   Price, $1.50.

VOLUME XLVI, 1911-1912. 623 pp. Price, cloth, $4.50.

1. [114] The Ricardian Socialists.   By ESTHER LOWENTHAL, Ph.D. Price, $1.00.
2. [115] Ibrahim Pasha, Grand Vizier of Suleiman, the Magnificent.
                                By HESTER DONALDSON JENKINS, Ph.D. Price, $1.00.
3. [116] *The Labor Movement in France. A Study of French Syndicalism.
                                By LOUIS LEVINE, Ph.D. Price, $1.50
4. [117]*A Hoosier Village.   BY NEWELL LEROY SIMS, Ph.D. Price, $1.50.

VOLUME XLVII, 1912. 544 pp. Price, cloth, $4.00.

1. [118] The Politics of Michigan, 1865-1878.
                                By HARRIETTE M. DILLA, Ph. D. Price, $2.00.
2. [119] *The United States Beet-Sugar Industry and the Tariff.
                                By ROY G. BLAKEY, Ph.D. Price, $2.00.

VOLUME XLVIII, 1912. 493 pp. Price, cloth, $4.00.

1. [120] Isidor of Seville.   By ERNEST BREHAUT, Ph. D. Price, $2.00.
2. [121] Progress and Uniformity in Child-Labor Legislation.
                                By WILLIAM FIELDING OGBURN, Ph.D. Price, $1.75.

VOLUME XLIX, 1912. 592 pp. Price, cloth, $4.50.

1. [122] British Radicalism 1791-1797.   By WALTER PHELPS HALL. Price, $2.00.
2. [123] A Comparative Study of the Law of Corporations.
                                By ARTHUR K. KUHN, Ph.D. Price $1.50.
3. [124] *The Negro at Work in New York City.
                                By GEORGE E. HAYNES, Ph.D. Price, $1.25

VOLUME L, 1912. 481 pp. Price, cloth, $4.00.

1. [125] The Spirit of Chinese Philanthropy.   By YAI YUE TSU, Ph.D. Price, $1.00.
2. [126] *The Alien in China.   By VI. KYUIN WELLINGTON KOO, Ph.D. Price, $2.50.

VOLUME LI, 1912. 4to. Atlas. Price : cloth, $1.50; paper covers, $1.00.

1. [127] The Sale of Liquor in the South.
                                By LEONARD S. BLAKEY, Ph.D.

VOLUME LII, 1912. 489 pp. Price, cloth, $4.00.

1. [128] *Provincial and Local Taxation in Canada.
                                By SOLOMON VINEBERG, Ph.D. Price, $1.50.
2. [129] *The Distribution of Income.   By FRANK HATCH STREIGHTOFF. Price, $1.50.
3. [130] *The Finances of Vermont.   By FREDERICK A. WOOD, Ph.D. Price, $1 00.

VOLUME LIII, 1912. 769 pp. Price, cloth, $4.50.

[131] The Civil War and Reconstruction in Florida.   By W. W. DAVIS. (*In press.*)

The price for each separate monograph is for paper-covered copies; separate monographs marked, can
be supplied bound in cloth, for 50c. additional. All prices are net.*

The set of fifty-three volumes, covering monographs 1-131, is offered, bound, for $172: except that
  Volume II can be supplied only in part, and in paper covers, no. 1 of that volume being out of print.
  Volumes I, III, IV and XXV, can now be supplied only in connection with complete sets.

For further information, apply to

Prof. EDWIN R. A. SELIGMAN, Columbia University,
or to Messrs. LONGMANS, GREEN & CO., New York.
London: P. S. KING & SON, Orchard House, Westminster.

Date Due